FINDING MY WAY

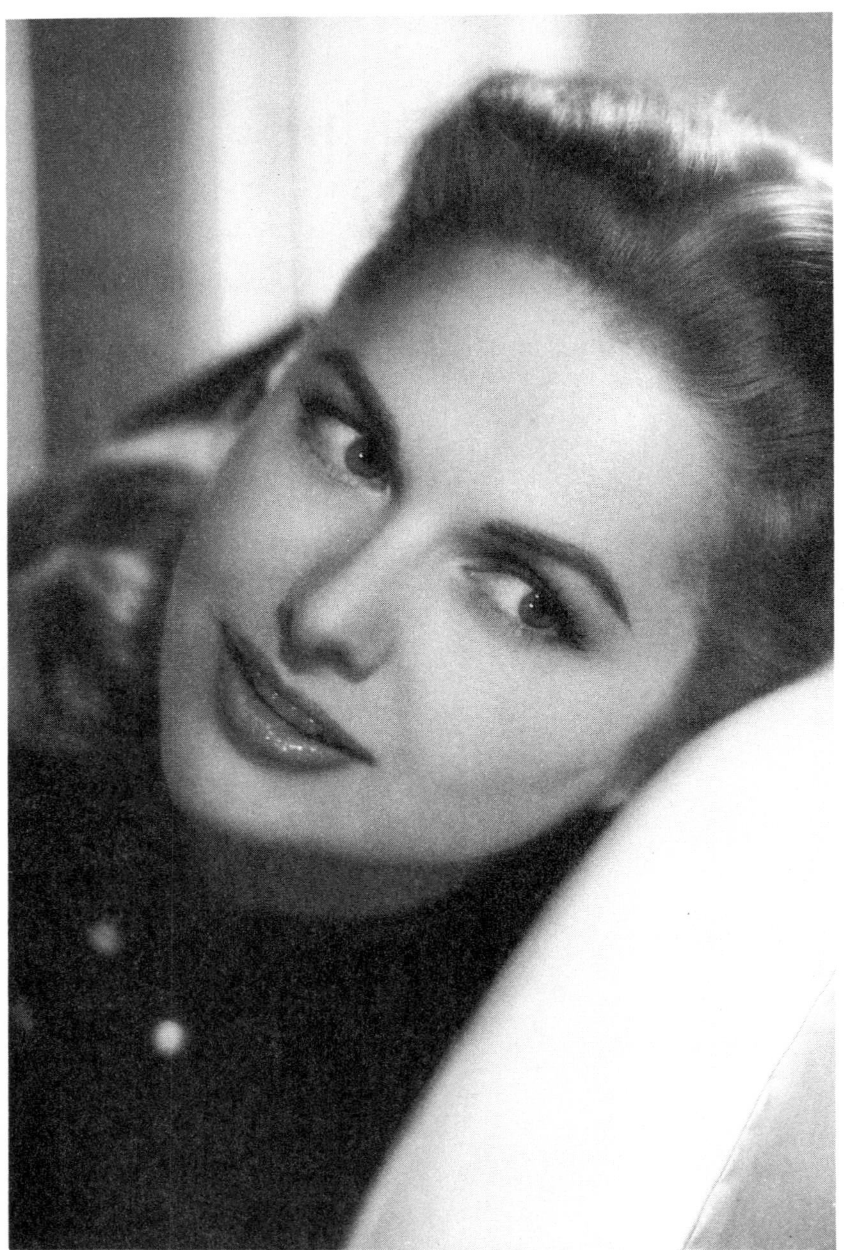

FINDING MY WAY

A Hollywood Memoir

Martha Hyer Wallis

HarperSanFrancisco
A Division of HarperCollins*Publishers*

Grateful acknowledgment is made for permission to quote excerpts from the following: *Starmaker*, by Hal Wallis and Charles Higham. Reprinted with permission of Macmillan Publishing Company. Copyright © 1980 by Hal Wallis and Charles Higham. *The Royal Road to Reality*, by Barbara Mary Muhl. Copyright © 1982 by Barbara Mary Muhl. Used with permission.

FIRST EDITION

Library of Congress Cataloging-in-Publication Data

Wallis, Martha Hyer.
Finding my way—a Hollywood memoir / Martha Hyer Wallis—1st ed.
p. cm.
ISBN 0-06-250938-1
1. Wallis, Martha Hyer. 2. Motion picture actors and actresses—United States—Biography. I. Title.
PN2287.W35A3 1990
791.43′028′092—dc20 90-32089
[B] CIP

90 91 92 93 94 HAD 10 9 8 7 6 5 4 3 2 1

This edition is printed on acid-free paper that meets the American National Standards Institute Z39.48 Standard.

With my gratitude to
Marion, Jane, and Oscar Dystel
for their encouragement,
enthusiasm,
and caring friendship

There is within us That which is the way.
Joel S. Goldsmith, *The World Is New*

CONTENTS

LIST OF ILLUSTRATIONS

For my work in *Some Came Running*, 1958, I was nominated for an Academy Award. Working with Frank Sinatra, Shirley MacLaine, and Vincente Minnelli was exciting.
Glamour portraits. bottom (photograph by John Engstead); top (courtesy of Paramount Pictures)
Cary Grant, *Houseboat*, 1958
Frank Sinatra, *Some Came Running*, 1958. Copyright© 1958 Loew's Inc. and Sol C. Siegel Productions, Inc. Ren. 1986 MGM/UA Entertainment Co. and Sol C. Siegel Productions, Inc. Courtesy of Turner Entertainment Co.
Tony Curtis, *Mister Cory*, 1957. Copyright © by Universal Pictures, a Division of Universal City Studios, Inc. Courtesy of MCA Publishing Rights, a division of MCA Inc.)
Danny Kaye, *The Man from the Diner's Club*, 1953. Courtesy of Columbia Pictures.
Marlon Brando, *The Chase*, 1966. Courtesy of Columbia Pictures.
Van Johnson, *Wives and Lovers*, 1963. Copyright © 1963 by Hal B. Wallis and Joseph H. Hazen. All rights reserved. Courtesy of Paramount Pictures.
John Wayne, *The Sons of Katie Elder*, 1965. Copyright © 1965 by Hal B. Wallis and Joseph H. Hazen, and John Wayne. All rights reserved. Courtesy of Paramount Pictures.
My real-life leading man, Hal Wallis
Life magazine, May 4, 1959 (Time Inc. Magazines)
Meeting the queen at the Royal Performance of Hal's *Anne of the Thousand Days*, 1969
With Hal, Katharine Hepburn, and John Wayne on location for *Rooster Cogburn*, Bend, Oregon, 1975
Santa Fe, 1985

All photos are from the author's collection, unless otherwise specified.

PREFACE

I know it's fashionable to write exposés of the seamy side of Hollywood lives, best-sellers that dwell upon the perverse and ugly world of scandalous relationships, drugs, and egocentricity. Such excessiveness did and does exist. But there is another Hollywood—where ordinary life goes on, where people whose faces are known worldwide buy extension cords in hardware stores and stop at convenience shops for cartons of milk on the way home from work.

From 1946 until 1986, I was a part of that life, subject to the same mixture of good and bad that exists in every community.

In Hollywood's "Golden Age," it was the responsibility of the studio public relations departments to produce images that hid the bad, emphasized the glamorous, and often overshadowed the human side of its citizens. I knew many stars and superstars who took great pains not to parade their acts of genuine humanity. When you live with fame as a day-to-day reality, the allure of privacy and anonymity is as strong as the desire for fame by those who have never had it.

This is a glimpse, hung on the story of one life, of what it was really like—the good and the bad.

But as will soon become evident, I learned that the good is the only reality that actually counts. I learned this late, at a moment of personal crisis, when caught in a web of self-destruction that took a lifetime to weave.

FINDING
MY
WAY

1

LOST-AND FOUND

11:00 P.M., January 1981,
Trancas Beach,
Malibu, California

I lay back against the Porthault patterned cushions of a wicker chaise on the balcony of our Trancas Beach house, staring out over a phosphorescent sea. Moonlight whitewashed the dunes, and the citrusy-sweet Santa Ana breeze gently dried my tearstained cheeks. I could hear faint laughter and vintage Sinatra from a party nearby. It was the perfect Hollywood setting for romance. I'd played the scene many times, but now the make-believe was over. This was the darkest night of my life.

My husband slept peacefully in his bedroom next to mine, but I couldn't sleep. My world was coming apart. Everything I'd lived and worked for was in jeopardy, and I faced the inescapable fact that I was responsible for my own undoing. I saw no way out of the abyss I'd fallen into. It was the lowest point of my life. Rock bottom.

There are all kinds of Gethsemanes: illness, addiction,

emotional despair. The most tragic are those we bring upon ourselves—avoidable heartbreak.

I closed my eyes and retraced the intricate pattern of my self-destruction. I'd had so much. My childhood was happy and carefree, full of Saturday matinees and Sunday school. I'd been given a good education, the finest training. That dreamed-of "break" in films had come early in my career. I'd married a wonderful man, and we had a near-perfect marriage.

Marrying Hal Wallis was the best thing that ever happened to me. Maybe because I loved my father so much, I'd looked all my life for a man smarter and stronger than I—someone I could look up to and respect. Hal was all that. He was a giant in the film industry and in life, a legend in his own time.

From an impoverished childhood in Chicago, Hal had worked his way up to become head of Warner Bros. Studio in the thirties and forties—the golden boy of a golden era. Most of the films he produced there are classics: *Dawn Patrol, The Maltese Falcon, Little Caesar, Yankee Doodle Dandy, Now Voyager,* and *Casablanca* among them.

After leaving Warner Bros., he became one of the first independent filmmakers—prolific, successful, revered. (And often feared. His temper was as legendary as his talent.) In the fifties and sixties, he produced such memorable films as *Come Back, Little Sheba, The Rose Tattoo, The Rainmaker, Gunfight at the OK Corral,* and *True Grit.* He discovered great stars, including Elvis Presley, Shirley MacLaine, Kirk Douglas, Burt Lancaster, Charlton Heston, Jerry Lewis, and Dean Martin.

I was proud to be his wife—so proud of his accomplishments that I sang his praises endlessly. He called me his best press agent.

Hal was twenty-six years older than I, tall, healthy, and handsome. He cultivated a year-round tan that contrasted dramatically with his salt-and-pepper hair and sky-blue eyes. He had a fine mind and a very special dry wit. There was an aura of strength and energy about him that was electric. Power is the greatest aphrodisiac, and most women found him irresistible. He was measured and calm unless provoked, dressed conservatively, did not smoke, drank little, was the complete antithesis of the potbellied, cigar-smoking stereotyped image of a Hollywood producer. He had class.

We were companions, friends as well as lovers. We liked the same things—fine food, travel, films, reading, television, quiet times. We laughed at the same things, were comfortable together.

The only problem in our relationship was money. It was the dark underside of our marriage, the somber underpainting of a brilliant canvas.

People laughed when we were married. They doubted it would last because our life-styles were so different.

Hal was known for his parsimony. His impoverished childhood in Chicago had made him frugal to the point of penny-pinching. "The only dollar Hal Wallis ever gave away" was framed and hung on a wall in the executive offices of Paramount Studios.

I, on the other hand, was known for my extravagance. My family had not been wealthy, but I was born profligate. As a child, I often spent my lunch money on the way to school. To quote my father: "Marty spends money like a drunken sailor." On the behavior-pattern side of my report card, teachers noted, "Does not appreciate the value of money." Oh, but I did, dear ladies. I believed even then that if you could buy beauty or comfort or pleasure at any price, it was a bargain. Money to me has always meant freedom to enjoy life.

Hal was in bondage to it. I never knew the extent of his fortune. He was so secretive about his finances that every business paper or joint tax return I signed was covered so that I couldn't read it—even parts of our prenuptial agreement were concealed.

The interminable arguments we had over bills were seeds sown early in our marriage that grew into my present life crisis. I teased Hal about his stinginess—even had a pillow embroidered, "It is better to live rich than to die rich." But after experiencing the famed Wallis temper and subsequent "cold treatment" on a day-to-day basis, I realized that if we were ever to be happy, the one subject we could never discuss was money.

For the first few years of our marriage, I personally financed our life-style with earnings from the fifty or sixty films I'd made before retiring to marry Hal. (I was told that his first wife solved similar problems the same way.) Peace at last. He never questioned how I managed to run three residences on the small allowance he gave me each month.

Hal kept abreast of the times in every other way, but moneywise he was in a time warp—fixed in the forties. He stubbornly refused to acknowledge how expensive the cost of living had become. He bragged to friends about how little he paid our help while I made up the difference in their actual salaries from my savings.

I paid for the lavish parties we gave, my clothes, our silver, crystal, and china, and many of the beautiful antiques and artifacts in our homes. I did not gamble, did not buy furs or jewelry, never looked at another man. But my tastes were extravagant. I wanted us to enjoy the best of everything, and we did.

My personal painting collection was traded up for some of the finer French Impressionistic paintings we acquired. I didn't mind. Love is giving and sharing, and I loved my husband very much.

Hal adored his new life-style. Before our marriage, he had been labeled a loner and a "grade-A recluse." After it, he entertained proudly in his beautiful homes, became active in community affairs, mellowed into a relaxed, gentler man.

But we were living in a house of cards. The dissimilarity of our values as far as money was concerned was a problem so real that it slowly began to unravel the strongly knit pattern of our happy lives. My funds ran out, and I borrowed heavily. As the bills piled up, I desperately borrowed more.

I justified my behavior by convincing myself that I was spending my inheritance from Hal while we could enjoy it together. What I couldn't face was the fact that—driven by pride, ambition, and vanity—I was gambling away the future to fulfill my insatiable desires. How had I become so obsessed with image? I wanted Hal to enjoy the kind of life a man in his position deserved. But at what cost? Seemingly, at any cost.

Banks do not lend large amounts of money to a wife without a husband's knowledge or consent, so I was forced to make choices I never dreamed I'd consider. I drove our Silver Cloud Rolls Royce into the seediest section of Los Angeles looking for loan sharks. The dregs of society—venal, cruel, corrupt—walked eagerly into my life.

I experienced the underworld, the terrifying dark side of reality. The people there were glad to lend me money. The payback on my initial loan of $100,000 was $350,000.

When I borrowed $350,000 to pay the $100,000, the payback on the new loan was $750,000. The figures soon escalated into millions. What should have been normal business became blackmail.

When I got behind in my payments, I was used ruthlessly. My signature was forged on documents I'd never seen. Loans that I knew nothing about were made in my name with my collateral. My home was plundered. I was caught in a maelstrom of illegal transactions, swindles, and felonies that drew me ever closer to disaster, even incarceration.

When the phone rang or the door bell chimed, I froze, panicked. Threatening letters arrived daily. Hal wondered why I was so jumpy. How could I tell him? He was a self-made man who prided himself on his integrity and financial security. Public disclosure of the sordid details of my injudiciousness could ruin him. And he would divorce me—of that I was sure.

I opened my eyes. A cool north wind blew clouds across the Malibu moon. Moving inside the house, I shivered more from fear than the chill.

The next day, my extortioners would demand their due. I could no longer pay them, and I knew Hal would never understand; no one would. I had dissipated all the great gifts of my life—for what? I was a fool and had only myself to blame for the destruction of everything I held dear.

In my bed, I cried out to God for help. I prayed to Him in the darkness every night of my life, but I needed Him in this darkest night as never before. Instead of asking, imploring, telling God what to do, I surrendered myself to Him completely.

Is this all there is, Lord?

Is this, then, what life is all about? Ambition, struggle, fear, running like rats on a wheel in a cage? Running nowhere. For once the goal is reached, the treadmill starts all over again in a different direction.

It's so empty, meaningless, a never-ending struggle for survival without any real purpose.

There has to be something more—something cleaner and better than humanhood.

I know You are there.

You've always been there.

But I'm afraid I tried to do it my way—not Yours—and I've made such a mess of things.

Forgive me. Take over now.

You lead my life, not I.

Your will—not mine.

I love You with all my being.

I give You me.

In humility I gave God access to my soul. And He took it.

My hands began to tingle; my body was suffused with the rapture of pure, absolute love. I was transported, consumed, no longer aware of form but only of joyous, exalted sensation—ecstasy. Brilliant white light filled the room and enveloped me. Gently but firmly my hands were forced up and pressed together into a prayer position over my body. I was no longer in control—overwhelmed by a wondrous rush of purity and sweetness. Glory poured through me.

Perfect peace followed—lightness of being, as if a great weight had been lifted from me. I felt comforted, loved, His. Transfixed, I realized I could only have been embraced by the power and presence of the living God.

My life would never again be the same.

2

BEGINNINGS

I was born August 10, 1924, in Fort Worth, Texas.

My childhood was a very happy one. I was never the prettiest or the smartest or the most talented, but I was patricianly attractive, intuitively bright, and very, very lucky. Lucky primarily to have been born of the genes of Agnes Barnhart and Julien C. Hyer—Superparents.

My father was tall, blonde, handsome—a Robert Redford look-alike. He was a South Carolinian, a graduate of Wofford College with a law degree from Georgetown University.

Mother was beautiful inside and out. She was petite, brunette, sensitive, and caring, a speech graduate of Northwestern University. Both were very special people.

They met under romantic circumstances during World

War I. She was in France with the Red Cross, and he was a captain in the artillery. An eyelock across a crowded mess hall led to a marriage that lasted fifty good years.

They settled in Texas, where he practiced law and she gave birth to three daughters: Agnes Ann, Martha, and Jeanne.

I was the middle daughter, but my father's substitute son—independent, headstrong, a character. I was told that if I kissed my elbow, I'd turn into a boy. It didn't work, but I ran with them on the street; had rubber-gun fights with them; played kick-the-can, baseball, and football; climbed trees; even had my hair cut in a boyish bob.

As a child, I remember rolling downhill in lush spring grass, savoring the smell of the loamy, damp earth; selling Kool-Aid from an orange-crate stand in front of our house; loving the softness of my mother's skin as she hugged me; collecting coat hangers in my little red wagon to sell to the local cleaners for pennies; the soothing sound of rain on the roof as I drank hot chocolate, snug in a nest of quilts in my bed; selling salve from door to door in a magazine contest to win a pony (getting a fountain pen instead); the pungent aroma of our local grocer's store, its dark wood floor ingrained with the fragrance of freshly ground coffee, cinnamon, apples, and mint; summer days—sunflowers, zinnias, butterflies, the smell of honeysuckle, rocking on the porch sipping tart lemonade, hand-fanning dry Texas air, watching cottonwood flakes drift lazily down like summer snow; summer nights—Texas-sized moons, lightning bugs glowing in the dark, stars so close they became friends; dreaming of hitting a home run at recess at South Hi Mount School; putting on plays and pet shows in the attic; the First Methodist Church and Sunday school; grace before meals; Bible study and prayers; taking turns with my sisters hand-freezing ice cream for Sunday dinner; learning all the words to "O Little Town of Bethlehem" in return for a football one Christmas; the haunting sound of train whistles in the night, imagining their destinations, imagining me there someday.

I traveled alone to South Carolina at the age of six to visit my grandparents. Railroad personnel took good care of me, and Mom prepared a beautiful basket of food that was to last me the trip. I finished it off the first hour out.

As I sat up in my berth at night behind heavy green Pullman curtains, eating candy bars and reading Big Little books, I felt I was LIVING. It could never get much better than that.

I liked traveling, and the following year decided to go to California to see my maternal grandparents. I packed my bag, stole a dime from the milkman's money, and walked to the streetcar stop with my six-year-old boyfriend. When the car came, he refused to get on, so I paid my fare, ran to the back of the car, and yelled "Yella, Yella" at him as we pulled away. About halfway to downtown Fort Worth (we lived in Arlington Heights), I asked the motorman to let me know when we reached California. He advised me to get off and return home, which I did. My frantic mother had called the police, my father had rushed home from work, and all were relieved and overjoyed when I limped in three hours later. I told them a very nice man had helped me carry my bag. When my anxious mother questioned this, I replied in a world-weary, know-everything tone, "Mother, I know he was nice. He had on a clean white shirt." (I had to live this down for the rest of my life. Every boyfriend I ever dated was judged by this criterion.)

I remember how supportive my parents were. When I represented our school in a relay race, my father took time off from his work to be in the stadium to watch me run. When I was in bed with a cold one Saturday, devastated because I couldn't see the latest episode of the serial *Riders of the Purple Sage,* Pop went to the theater in my place, brought me home a chocolate malt, and acted out all the action and dialogue so that I'd be in the know the next Saturday.

He was there in the audience when I lost in the finals of the citywide declamation contest, there in the car afterward to comfort and explain how important it is to try, to be a contender and either a good winner or a good loser—bittersweet words of wisdom I had cause to remember many times in my life.

My father and I went to baseball games together, ate hot dogs and rooted for the Fort Worth Cats. One season he promised to take me to Georgia for the Dixie Series if the Cats got into the play-offs. They didn't, but they were *our team.*

I loved Westerns. Tom Mix was my favorite star, and I prayed every night that someday I'd grow up to be a cowgirl. (Years later, under contract to RKO and stuck interminably in "B" Westerns, I used to shake my head and mutter, "He heard me. He heard me.")

My mother was a marvel, the glue that held us together. She was always there for us—day and night, TLC. She was the first up in the morning and the last to bed at night—did all the cooking, washing, sewing, teaching, loving.

She became active in the Camp Fire Girls so that we might benefit. We went on hikes and cookouts at Mary's Creek. One day we'd planned a picnic, and it rained. She had the picnic for us anyway, on an old quilt in front of a gas burner inside the house.

She was so resourceful, so inventive that we never knew we were growing up in the depression. She made tuna in real seashells so attractive and delicious that we clamored for it (that way she fed a family of five with one tin—ten cents in those days).

My father was international president of the Lions Clubs. Whenever he had a meeting at night and couldn't come home for dinner, Mom would say, "Surprise! We don't have to eat in the dining room tonight. We'll have baked potatoes around the stove in the kitchen." A treat.

She made a game out of passing along clothes from sister to sister, changing each outfit to make it suit the personality of the new owner.

She taught inspiration—that dreams do come true, that if you believe you can do something, you can. "Girlies," she counseled, "when you have to go without things, splurge on dreams. Never stop dreaming or believing you can do anything you set your mind and heart to." If a face is all that one can see of the soul, hers was the reflection of a very beautiful one. We all adored her.

During the depression, clients paid my father's legal fees with whatever they had to trade: turkeys, sausage, car repairs. Leon B. Lewis paid his bill with a family pass to his movie theater, The New Liberty. It was my ticket to the future.

Every Saturday in the dark theater, my sisters and I escaped to worlds far from the Texas plains. We flew down to Rio with Ginger and Fred, ate Italian in New York City with Alice Faye and Tyrone Power, sailed on art deco ocean liners, learned about emotions, life-styles, and situations we never knew existed. Movies were magic, our passport to outside. They were what our dreams were made of.

Naturally I wanted to be an actress. I never told any of my friends because I knew the idea was laughable. I was tall, skinny, adolescently awkward, with braces on my teeth and no figure. I did confide in my mother. She said, "But, Marty, I thought you wanted to be an artist." My answer: "Mom, nobody applauds when you paint."

In school, I tried out for every play, entered declamation contests and debates, joined the drama club. I knew exactly what I wanted and where I was going.

One night at an outdoor slumber party with three of my preteen girl friends, I almost gave away my secret. We lay on quilts under a windmill and a sky full of huge Texas stars, listening to big-band music and fantasizing about our futures. They described what kind of husbands they wanted, the kind of life each would have. I started to confide in them but then said nothing. I kept my dreams to myself—nourished them. I didn't want them ridiculed. From another world, a radio announcer signed off "from high atop Nob Hill in beautiful San Francisco." Lying in the Texas moonlight, I vowed I'd be there someday.

Every summer, our family traveled by car to Whittier, California, to visit relatives. My sisters and I were so movie struck that we made Mother's life miserable until she took us to the Hollywood Bowl or broadcasting studios where we might see stars. Incidentally, never at any time did I aspire to a career on the New York stage. I wanted to be a movie star, period.

I stood alone one night on the roof garden of the Highland Hotel looking out over the lights of Hollywood, playing the scene that has become a cliché only because aspiring actresses have always played it and always will. "Someday," I promised myself, "someday I'll be a part of it. I'll be back—and I'll make it. This is where I belong." Janet Gaynor may have done it better in *A Star Is Born,* but my dedication was just as heartfelt, just as fervent.

Determination burned in me like a flame. I lived a normal life, but all I thought about was someday—and Saturdays. Saturdays meant double features, magic carpet time.

Friends from school had their hair done on Saturdays, bought dollar lipsticks, and saw first-run movies at the Worth or Hollywood theaters uptown. My mother washed my hair, I could only afford ten-cent Tangee lipstick, and the movies we saw were second run in a lower-class section of town. It didn't matter a bit. I never felt deprived. I wasn't. I knew this was preparation, beginnings. I splurged on dreams.

In 1940, my life was every girl's fantasy of what high school should be: dates, dances, sorority meetings, football games, pep rallies. I kept up my grades, but what interested me most was what took place between classes—flirting, passing notes, relationships.

One memorable day, I had cause to remember my father's counsel on losing. At one time, he had been a Texas state senator in Austin and was then running for congessman from our district. My sisters and I passed out cards at political rallies and tried very hard to ignore the slanderous newspaper campaign waged against all candidates but the incumbent. On election night, the results indicated a runoff between my father and that man. Pop realized it would be an expensive and losing proposition and regretfully conceded the race. The headline in the next morning's *Fort Worth Star Telegram* read, "HYER QUITS!"

I held my head high in school that day, ignoring the stares and jokes and jeers. Inwardly, my heart was breaking for my father. Outwardly, I smiled and pretended I'd never had a bad day in my life, which absolutely infuriated my hecklers.

Coming home from a dance one night in my senior year of high school, I was in an automobile accident that has affected me ever since. It was raining, and the car skidded into a telephone pole—no drinking, no drugs, just an oil-slicked Camp Bowie Boulevard.

My date and I were in the backseat. I leaned forward to warn the driver, but the brakes locked in the skid. As we hit the pole, I smashed into the back of the front seat, bending it into an inverted V.

In the eerie postcrash quiet, I remember seeing blood streaming down the face of the girl in the front seat. She had hit the windshield and was cut very badly. In shock, I felt blood on my own face and in my mouth. I knew I had been cut, too. I couldn't move my right leg.

As I was lifted onto a stretcher in the rain, an ambulance attendant asked if I had a choice of hospitals.

"Yes," I whispered. "Cook."

I had never been in it but had admired Cook, the most beautiful hospital in town and also the most expensive. Later, when the bills had finally been paid, my father joked (on the square), "Marty, dear, I pray there will never be a next time. But if so, please whisper 'Methodist.'"

I suffered a crushed right knee, severed ligaments in the leg, cuts on my face that required five stitches, and internal complications.

Strangely enough, I hadn't wanted to go out that night. But as a sponsor of the dance, I was obligated to be there. Sitting in my formal, waiting for my date, I'd told Mother of my foreboding. Something didn't feel right, I told her—I wished I didn't have to go. She remembered that later. When the phone rang at midnight, my father answered it, but she had already started dressing. She knew. She told me every parent's dread is that shrill telephone ring in the dark when the children are out. It means only one thing—trouble.

For six months, I recuperated in the hospital and at home, taking a quantum leap into maturity. Growing-up time.

The music had stopped. All the things that seemed so important to me as a superficial teenager no longer mattered. I began to realize for the first time how much we need each other, how much we need faith in a power greater than our very fragile selves.

Every Sunday of my short life, I had been taken to church and had recited the works of worship by rote. My concept of God then was a gray-bearded presence in the sky who rewarded goodness and punished badness like Santa Claus. I expected Him to do my will, fulfill my desires. I tried to make deals with Him. Now I promised Him everything and anything if I could be healthy like everyone else. I'd be so good if I could just walk normally. I'd never complain again.

For life had gone on without me. Bedridden, I'd watched my friends drift away one by one, too busy to visit as the months went by. I was old news.

Doctors scheduled complicated knee surgery with a 50–50 chance of success. If the operation worked, my knee would work. If it failed, my knee would be stiff the rest of my life. Thankfully, my parents chose not to have the surgery done.

When the cast was finally removed, I was horrified. My leg had wasted away to skin and bones and was covered with long black unshaved hair. Mom massaged it with hot oil morning and night. I walked on crutches for months and with a cane and a pronounced limp for years.

I still have chips of bone floating around in my knee. My leg gives way occasionally and painfully forecasts damp weather. It is slightly bowed and lumpy, but it works.

The fact that I could walk at all was a miracle. Doctors credited my healing to youth and luck. Very privately, I credited it to God.

I went back to school on crutches with an awareness and understanding of the human condition far beyond my sixteen years. I was a different person, a better person—less self-centered, less inclined to play games flaunting my newly found feminine power. After facing the concept of death as a reality for the first time, I valued life as never before and began to ponder its meaning. Seeds were planted.

3

PURSUING THE DREAM: HOLLYWOOD

When I graduated from high school in June 1941, most of the world was at war, and America was preparing for it. As a major in the army reserve, my father was stationed at Fort Sam Houston in San Antonio, Texas, and our family moved there to be with him.

That fall, I enrolled in Fairfax Hall Junior College for Girls on a scholastic scholarship. The school was in the Blue Ridge Mountains of Virginia, an area so breathtakingly beautiful I found it hard to study. Having never experienced the seasons, I was spellbound by the splendor of fall foliage, snow, spring blossoms, and lush green summers—the theology of nature.

Fairfax was so different from public high school in Texas. There were only six girls in some of my classes. Instruction was individual and special. I had daily therapy for my leg in a heated pool. Military schools and colleges were nearby, and every weekend there were chaperoned dances at VMI (Virginia Military Institute), VPI (Virginia Polytechnic Institute), Staunton, and the University of Virginia. I loved it.

In the drama department, I was given the opportunity to play roles I'd never have played elsewhere; I could experiment. I grew there. Fairfax Hall inspired me, and later Northwestern University honed and toughened me—little time and big time. Both were very necessary to my development as a person and as a performer.

Speech classes at Fairfax were held in a primitive loft over the gymnasium. The only decoration was a framed picture of Katharine Hepburn, our inspiration.

One of my proudest possessions is the Fairfax Hall Honor Medal. "A winner of this medal must stand high, though not necessarily highest in her class work. The medal signifies that the winner has shown a spirit of loyalty to the ideals that we hope may ever be incorporated in the traditions of Fairfax Hall."

Many of the girls at Fairfax were army brats and navy juniors. One Sunday morning in December, my roommate and I heard screams and sobbing in the hall outside our room. The news of the bombing of Pearl Harbor had just come over the radio, and the girls with fathers stationed there were terrified. Most of them left school immediately.

The war changed all our lives. My father was made a full colonel and sent overseas. He served on the staffs of Generals Donovan, Lucas, Gerow, and Patton. He saw battle service in the Ardennes and Rhineland campaign, was awarded several decorations, and was instrumental in setting up the first war crimes trials while serving as judge advocate of the Fifteenth Army.

I finished two idyllic years at Fairfax Hall, then enrolled as a junior in the School of Speech at Northwestern University, Evanston, Illinois.

That was life in the fast lane—competitive, impersonal, tough. Some of my classes numbered two hundred students, and you were known by your seat section rather than by a name. Curiously enough, I thrived on it. For the first time, I *learned* what I was being taught rather than just memorizing to get good grades.

Most of the college-age male population was at war, but the all-girl student body didn't lack for dates. We had V-12 units training on campus and hometown boyfriends to write to and see on leave.

I pledged Pi Phi and lived at the sorority house, but baby-sat on weekends and worked part-time at Billy Boy Candies and Stevens Department Store to help pay my way. My parents were not wealthy, but they saw to it that their three girls had college educations. How they did it I'll never know, but I was grateful for the sacrifices they were making for me. I did what I could to help.

Incidentally, my parents had promised us a trip to Europe if we didn't smoke, drink, or get married until after we were twenty-one. None of us did. Unfortunately, they couldn't afford to send us, but they ended up with three very nice girls. And we've been catching up ever since!

I remember the frigid winds off Lake Michigan as I walked to classes at Northwestern, and trips on the "L" into Chicago's Loop to see movies—*Casablanca, Now Voyager, Yankee Doodle Dandy*—never dreaming I would someday be married to the man who made them.

I was the Pi Phi candidate for Navy Ball Queen, but I lost. I was not even a runner-up. I was devastated and felt that I had let my friends down. But it was just not my time. I was unsophisticated, unprepared to compete with city girls with professional hair styling and designer clothes. I wore no makeup but lipstick, I washed and set my own hair, and my ball gown had been made by a little country dressmaker in Texas. Not good enough. This was Chicago—the big time. There was no one to comfort me that midnight after the ball, no loving parents to remind me it's what's inside that counts. I walked the shores of Lake Michigan licking my wounds, renewing my spirit, still having to splurge on dreams.

With the money I'd earned, I enrolled in the summer session of the Pasadena Playhouse in California. I knew it was a fine showcase. I could live there in the girls' dormitory and continue my training while evaluating the Hollywood scene. It would give me a base to work from. I wouldn't be part of the great, invading horde arriving with no experience, no money, no immediate chance of employment, and no place to stay. Five days after graduation, I spent my savings on a one-way ticket to Pasadena and boarded the Sunshine Special whistling "California, Here I Come."

The first morning at the Playhouse, an instructor informed us in no uncertain terms that we were there to study and work—to forget about our dreams of being whisked off to Hollywood in a limousine, signing a fabulous contract, and starring overnight in a colossal Technicolor opus. It just wasn't going to happen.

He was right. Instead, we painted scenery, sewed costumes, improved our diction, learned to improvise—and longed to appear in the very professional main stage productions.

My chance finally came. I got a small but very showy part in a modern comedy. I spent the rest of my savings on an Adrian suit to wear onstage and sent free tickets for the performance to every agent and talent scout I'd read about in the movie magazines.

This was it. I'd find out if I had it.

The pressure built through readings, rehearsals, dress rehearsal. The night finally arrived. But instead of facing an enthusiastic audience of interested theatergoers, we played to an empty house.

It was V-J night, and the country was going wild. The war was over! Even the streets of staid Pasadena were full of honking cars, music, strangers kissing strangers. Stores closed. At a soda fountain that afternoon, I had been given a hot fudge sundae on the house. It was bedlam. A whole new world, with democracy triumphant.

Meanwhile, back at the Playhouse, we gave our all to an empty theater. And the performance was scheduled for one night only. Fate.

The following week, I appeared in one of the Greek classics as an old beggar with a beard. When the curtain came down, a very quiet little man came backstage and asked to see me. He said his name was Milton Lewis. He was a talent scout from Paramount Studios and he liked the energy and enthusiasm I had displayed on stage. He wanted me to come to the studio the next day to do a reading for his casting people. I was so thrilled that even the warnings of Playhouse pros that such an interview meant little or nothing couldn't dampen my spirits.

The next day, after an hour-long bus ride, I read from *The White Cliffs of Dover* in the fishbowl at Paramount (a tinted glass room designed so that the executives could see you but you couldn't see them). I was told they would get in touch with me at a later date, studio production had fallen off, they weren't making any screen tests, and so forth.

I knew I was being brushed off, but my foot had been in the door. They had nibbled—and I was hooked.

When the summer session at the playhouse ended, I was able to rent a room in a private home in Hollywood for twenty-five dollars a month. My funds were running low, so I took a temporary job selling pots and pans in Kress's basement on Hollywood Boulevard. It required no experience or dedication, and I would be relatively free to go on interviews.

I quickly discovered the catch-22 of the film business: you can't work in a picture unless you are a member of the Screen Actor's Guild (SAG), and you can't join the guild unless you have a part in a film. And most of the newspaper ads for "actress wanted" meant you'd be taken for expensive photos or much worse.

But my spirits were high. In those days, Hollywood Boulevard was fun—nice stores, restaurants, theaters. Every noon, I ate a candy bar and an apple on a bench in the forecourt of the Egyptian Theater and daydreamed of attending premieres there.

I was a good girl. I wrote home once a week and attended church every Sunday. I church-shopped by bus, looking for the right message, the right messenger for me. I found both in the spirit of the great Dr. Louis Evans, pastor of the Hollywood Presbyterian Church. His sermons were powerful, unforgettable.

By this time, my father was judge advocate of the Fifteenth Army in Bad Nauheim, Germany. I had written him about my "break" at the playhouse and how I was following it up on my own in Hollywood. As luck would have it, Ella Logan, the Scotch songstress, came to Bad Nauheim to entertain the troops. While seeing Pop about red tape concerning her tour, she saw my picture prominently displayed on his desk. Very graciously, she cabled her producer husband in California to see me.

I'll never forget the day I took the bus to 20th Century Fox Studios to meet him. This is how I described it in a letter to my family:

> I shopped all day yesterday in downtown Los Angeles and finally found the grey flannel suit I wanted and a cloche hat to match. (Plus a *wonderful* new girdle at Robinson's that does away completely with my hips.) It took all my money—$50.00—but I'm gambling it will be worth it.
>
> Today I put on my new outfit—with a single strand of my best fake pearls and white gloves, my Chen Yu Cloudstick makeup and Chen Yu Dragon's Blood red lipstick—and set off to seek my fortune at 20th Century Fox. (My new permanent is the best I've ever had—nice and fluffy and soft. I part it on the side now and wear it long and bouncy.)
>
> Anyway, the studio is halfway to Santa Monica and although it was 95° today I wasn't uncomfortable until I got there. Then I was shaking!
>
> The studio is immense. In front, there's a large white building of executive offices, and that's where I was directed to go. The reception desk is out of this world—knotty pine with inset pictures of their stars and real flowers all around.
>
> After the policeman went through the formalities, he let me in and I went up to the third floor past all the famous directors' offices—even Darryl F. Zanuck's.
>
> Mr. Finklehoff was expecting me and was so nice, but I almost burst into tears when he advised me to

go back home, marry the boy next door, and have a large family. As I was leaving—holding my head high—an important-looking man stopped me in the hall and introduced himself. He was Frank Orsatti. I remembered reading about him in the movie magazines. He is a very powerful agent. He gave me his card and asked me to come see him tomorrow in his offices on the Sunset Strip! He told me that I'm the least Hollywood-looking girl he's seen in a long time. "You look like you're going to a tea in Dallas. I want to take you to RKO looking just the way you do right now," he said. I don't think I'll be able to sleep tonight I'm so excited. I feel like Scarlett O'Hyer. Hurry, tomorrow!

And that's how it happened. The next morning, I found myself in the offices of Charles Koerner, the production head of RKO. Mr. Koerner felt I had "class" and, although I was *very* raw material, might possibly be molded into something different from the run-of-the-mill starlet. He was willing to gamble $150 a week for six months on a stock contract to see how I developed. "Good luck," he said. Handshake, end of interview.

I left his office in a daze. I couldn't believe it.

Mr. Orsatti walked me over to the publicity department to introduce me to Perry Leiber, and en route we passed Cary Grant. "Hey, Cary," Frank called. "Meet Martha Hyer. She's going to be your leading lady someday." Cary smiled politely. I cringed with embarrassment, but Frank was right. Twenty years later, Cary and I made *Houseboat* together. (I was a late bloomer!)

RKO became my finishing school. I served my apprenticeship there. I learned my craft. I had drama lessons every day with Lillian Albertson, the studio coach; worked out in the gym for body training; and became the star of the still gallery. Through my good friend Arlene Jost of the publicity department, I learned how I photographed best, what kind of makeup suited me, how to wear my hair, how to dress to flatter my figure.

I felt I was part of a family. In the studio system, everyone on the lot was *for* you. I found an undertone of kindness and warmth in the Hollywood of those days that I have never forgotten, maybe because it was so unexpected.

Stock players worked constantly, either in a film or for the publicity department or doing personal appearances. Every department in the studio was dedicated to getting the names and faces of the players better known.

I was given bit parts in several pictures that I see on cable TV today. It's unbelievable to go back in time—to see my mugging brunette young self trying too hard to make an impression with a one-line bit. I'm surprised the directors didn't give me the hook.

My first starring role was the lead in a low-budget Western opposite Tim Holt—*Thunder Mountain*. I was Little Nell in lots of those Westerns. Then I graduated to featured roles in "A" movies like *Roughshod, The Judge Steps Out,* and *The Velvet Touch.*

Roughshod was a Western starring Gloria Grahame, Robert Sterling, and Claude Jarman, Jr. (of *The Yearling* fame). I played a supporting role. It was filmed on location near Bridgeport, California, and was one of Mark Robson's first directorial efforts. It was a big-budgeted picture, and I was thrilled to be a part of it. We lived in a tent city in the mountains.

The altitude wasn't a problem, but I didn't feel well. I was afraid it might show in my work, so I asked the first-aid man on the set for help. He diagnosed my upset stomach and dry heaves as indigestion and prescribed a laxative, the worst possible medication for my condition, appendicitis.

My temperature soared. I was feverish, swollen, comatose. It became obvious that without an immediate operation, I faced a ruptured appendix.

The operation took place in a first-aid station high in the Sierras. It was right out of a Marx brothers film but could easily have been tragic. I had to sign a paper relieving the studio of all responsibility if the operation proved fatal or incapacitating.

The surgeon was a retired doctor who had a fishing cabin in the area. His operating table was a chest of drawers with two quilts on top. He gave me a local anesthetic to ease the pain, then started cutting. He whistled while he worked and attempted to carry on a conversation, as if we were at a social event. Very "M*A*S*H." "Do you like to dance?" he asked. Then he said, "Uh-oh," in a guilty tone, indicating he'd made a mistake or that something was wrong.

I kept my eyes tightly shut and prayed. I urged the doctor to hurry as the anesthetic was wearing off. At one point, he asked his lady friend (who was assisting) for a roll of gauze. She said she thought he had it. He said he thought she had it. We waited while she climbed a ladder to get it off a top shelf.

After the surgery, I was taken to a high-country hospital (four beds) to recuperate. I stayed there for a sleepless week. The lady in the bed on one side of me drank from a hidden bottle and had hallucinations. The occupant of the bed on the other side screamed in pain, reliving the accident in which she'd been injured.

None too soon, RKO transported me back to Hollywood in an ambulance. The director shot around me in the picture until I was well enough to work.

Some of the pictures I did at RKO were dreadful, but they were good experience. My theory has always been that you're only an actress if you act. The more you do, the better your chances are of finding that one great role that is going to be a breakthrough.

Part of our training was to observe stars and directors at work on top films shooting on the lot. I sat spellbound watching Hitchcock direct Ingrid Bergman and Cary Grant in *Notorious*—and heard for the first time a now-classic Hitchcock story making the rounds. It seems that for *Lifeboat*, starring Tallulah Bankhead, most of the action was shot onstage in a mock-up of a boat reached by climbing a steep ladder. After several days of shooting, the assistant director came to Hitchcock with the embarrassing information that since Miss Bankhead did not wear panties under her dress, the crew was becoming quite intimately acquainted with her as she climbed in and out of the lifeboat. Hitchcock thought for a few minutes, then deadpanned, "Well, I can't decide if it's a problem for wardrobe, makeup, or hairdressing."

One Sunday, Mr. Orsatti called and invited me to a brunch at his beach house. He said it might help my career—give me a chance to be seen by people from other studios.

His chauffeur picked me up after church and drove me to Santa Monica. I wore a high-necked dress with white collar and cuffs, white halo hat, and white gloves. Baby Martha.

When I was ushered onto the beach patio, the informally dressed, very sophisticated guests took one look and as a group sighed "Awwwww." I think one of them even said,

"Get her a glass of milk, Frank." I sat quietly, looked, and listened. Even if I'd known what to say, I wouldn't have had a chance in that group.

The very young, very beautiful Gabor sisters sat across the table from the great director Mike Curtiz, Steve Trilling, and a tanned, handsome man who was the production head of Warner Bros. Studios, Hal Wallis. Linda Christian swam in the pool most of the time to show off her fantastic figure. After the guests left, I stayed for a while and watched Mr. Orsatti and his gofers play gin and listen to race results. When I was given permission to leave, the chauffeur drove me home. Many years later, I married Hal Wallis and teased him about giving Linda Christian a ride home that afternoon. He didn't remember me at all.

When RKO contract players were not working in a film or for the publicity department, we were often asked to visit veterans' hospitals in the area or assist with fund-raising for the Motion Picture Relief Fund Home.

Few people know that a percentage of all film salaries goes to the Motion Picture Relief Fund to take care of the ill and aging. The idea was born sixty-three years ago around a luncheon table at the Los Angeles Brown Derby. Mary Pickford, Charles Chaplin, and Douglas Fairbanks were discussing the financial plight of some of the aging men and women they had worked with. They put together a benevolent fund to give actors who need it a home where they can live in dignity and comfort. Those who can afford to pay do so. For others, it is free.

The Home has grown from the simple establishment where we starlets poured tea and carried trays in the forties to a beautiful ranch-type compound in Woodland Hills, California. Resortlike, with individual cottages, a theater, a library, and sports facilities, it is fully equipped to give the finest in medical care and TLC. Mary Astor and Norma Shearer spent the last years of their lives there.

Most film executives and stars are self-made successes. They show their gratitude by sharing generously with those less fortunate. From early on, I was well aware that the overprivileged in Hollywood never forget the underprivileged. Rosalind Russell proved that.

I first met this great lady making regular rounds at a children's hospital, lending moral and financial support to an organization she helped found.

She became a source of inspiration to me, on screen and off. I played a small part with her in *The Velvet Touch.* The help she gave me with my scenes was invaluable. I learned about camera angles from her, timing, how to hit my marks on the floor without looking at them. (After seeing a scene rehearsed, the lighting cameraman marks each actor's moves and positions with pieces of tape on the floor. Stand-ins are lit in those positions. If a player does not hit his mark in the "take," he is in the dark, not lit properly, and the scene has to be reshot.) Roz was completely professional yet made me feel she cared about me personally. I was not just another actress in a scene.

The whole studio cheered her fight to get the Sister Kenny film made. She worked for six years to put the story on the screen, to portray this woman she so admired. Her efforts helped put polio on the front pages and brought the Salk vaccine to a grateful world.

Rosalind Russell and her husband, Freddie Brisson, were very kind to me socially. They invited me to their home and introduced me to their friends.

It was always fun to be around Roz. Her sense of humor was infectious, her spirit indomitable. When she developed a severe case of rheumatoid arthritis, she did not let it defeat her. She went public in her efforts to lick the disease. She helped other sufferers by demonstrating that you can learn to live with arthritis and still be a part of life. I attended meetings with her as she crusaded for arthritis research, her gnarled fingers covered by high-fashion gloves that matched her Galanos gowns. She was always up, always smiling—Auntie Mame—never afraid of anything. She told me she thought of God as her friend.

There was warmth and fun and friendliness in film-making in the forties and fifties. Studio people were tightly knit units of hardworking, loyal, family-oriented folks. They loved what they were doing and took pride in their work. They were professionals and felt valued and special, knowing their individual contribution to the finished product was all-important. There was a wonderful sense of camaraderie—a comradeship—among film crew members. Let no one tell you Hollywood has no heart. I can still feel the warmth of its embrace.

I was under contract to RKO for three years and will always be grateful for the training I received. I feel sorry for young actors today who don't get that kind of grooming. It was of inestimable value. Years later, when I made films abroad, I was told that the "old" American film actors were the most disciplined in the world—were always cooperative, were on time, knew their dialogue, took direction well. That was stock contract training, gone forever with the studio system.

4

WOMAN OF THE WORLD

In 1948, Howard Hughes bought RKO and began what was called "the most insane era" in the company's history. Three-fourths of the studio work force was laid off. Production was cut to an absolute minimum. All contracts were cancelled at option time, including mine.

It was the beginning of very lean times for me. Jobs were few and far between in 1949 as the government "consent decree" forced studios to split theaters off from the production-distribution end of the business—the prime factor in the eventual collapse of the studio system.

As a free-lance actress, I managed to keep my little one-bedroom apartment by eating less and riding the bus to interviews instead of taking a taxi. I came to depend on the twenty-five dollars a week I received in government unemployment compensation as a lifeline.

But I hated feeling poor. Sometimes I'd march straight from the pay window of the Social Security office on Orange Drive to Hollywood Boulevard. There I'd spend most of my check for a steak and a salad at Musso and Franks, a box of See's candy, all the new movie magazines, and a ticket to whatever was playing at Grauman's Chinese Theater.

I went on lots of interviews and got some bit parts (rent payers—answered prayers), but nothing was really happening. Mr. Orsatti had died years before, and I couldn't find another agent who believed in me the way he had. I held my head high, wrote letters to my family about how well I was doing, and kept on.

Without realizing it, I became preoccupied with my own lack and fear. One evening, a good friend said to me, "You know, every time another actress is mentioned, you knock her. She's either fat or old or phony or something. You never say anything nice about anybody." Stunned, I knew he was right. It was true. I was so insecure, so jealous of others' success, I tried to bring them down to my level by belittling them. It was a lesson learned that I never forgot.

On an interview one day, the casting director flipped a coin to cast the role—heads, I got the part; tails, the other actress did. It fell heads, and as the other girl gathered up her things, she said, "Okay. That's it. I'm getting out of this business. It's too heartbreaking. After years of study and work, if that's the way a part can be cast, I've had it." She later became a very important television producer.

The road got rockier, but I persevered. Never once did I think of quitting—until I met C. Ray Stahl.

He was the son of Sennett bathing beauty Roxanna McGowan and silent film star Charles Ray. He was adopted by his stepfather, famous director John M. Stahl.

Ray's sister brought us together on a blind date, and we clicked. He had graduated from Stanford University, had served in the navy as a lieutenant on a destroyer in the Pacific, and was then working as a writer learning the film business. He lived with his parents in a wing of their lovely home on Nîmes Road in Bel Air and was the apple of his mother's eye. He was bright, witty, nice—an undervalued commodity in the mating game.

I liked Ray's friends, and they liked me. Ray and I had a wonderful time with the younger social set of Los Angeles. We went to parties, saw football games (even the Rams in the rain), played canasta, went sailing, saw movies, went to the track and to the fights—had a carefree, exciting courtship.

John Stahl was a very important director at 20th Century Fox, and Mrs. Stahl was an elegant, socially prominent lady who entertained beautifully. The guest lists of their parties read like a *Who's Who* of Hollywood.

At one of the Stahl dinners, I came face-to-face with my first artichoke. Having no idea what to do with it, I chattered away nervously with my dinner partners, watching their moves out of the corner of my eye. I managed, but barely. There had been no artichokes for me in cowtown.

At the track, Mr. Stahl bought tickets on every horse in every race to slip under my plate so I'd win enough to buy clothes for their parties.

It was in this period of my life that I first began to become materially minded. Clothes, cars, houses, possessions seemed very important to me. Too important. The Stahls' life-style became mine, and I'm afraid I fell headlong into the trap of desire and stayed there for many, many years. A wise man once said, "The world is won by those who let it go." I had to live a lifetime to learn the truth of that.

I wanted it all, and I was determined to have it. Ray gave me a beautiful engagement ring, and the future looked bright. It was to be the best time of our lives together.

In the late forties, Ray met George Breakston, and they formed a partnership to produce films globally.

Fate and *Geisha Girl* were made in Japan. Ray wrote and directed the pictures, and George produced them in collaboration with Toho Studios in Tokyo. I was the female lead in both films. They were not memorable, but the experience was. We lived in Japan for about a year. It was just after the war and a very exciting time to be there.

On the trip over, our camera equipment was bumped off the plane in Anchorage, Alaska, to make room for top-priority government cargo. Kegs shaped like little beer barrels were stored under our seats. The next morning, we were told they contained a million and a half dollars' worth of gold bullion being shipped to General Chiang Kai-shek on Formosa.

The plane refueled in Shemya in the Aleutian Islands. It was a barren outpost devoid of anything but an airstrip and a few Quonset huts. Inspired by *Mr. Roberts,* the men stationed there had put up signs reading "Ten Miles to the Tree," "Tread softly, you are approaching the Tree." The tree itself was pitiful, but carefully roped off and attended.

I'll never forget seeing sunrise over Fujiyama as we flew into Tokyo for the first time—a papier-mâché city after the B-29 bombings; sleeping under futons on straw tatami floors after hot mineral baths in a small country inn in Nikko; the incredible politeness of the Japanese people; sitting on the floor at geisha parties eating exquisitely prepared food as lovely Japanese girls in ceremonial kimonos performed traditional dances to the haunting music of a plucked stringed instrument from another age; seeing *Showboat* at the Ernie Pyle Theater in Tokyo, loving it, and being homesick for the States, for Hollywood, and for that type of professional filmmaking—would I ever be part of it again?; barely keeping a straight face when Japanese friends (who had difficulty pronouncing their *l*'s in English) assured us that in the presidential race, "We pray for General MacArthur's erection"; refusing to use the mixed rest rooms (men and women, no doors on the stalls) at the studio or at the office. At that time, people thought nothing of using them together. They thought nothing of using the street for the same purpose.

Because every available inch of land in Japan is used to grow food, dirt and fertilizer are very valuable commodities. When we were there, human fertilizer was gathered each night in central sewer stations all over Tokyo. In the mornings, we saw hundreds of carts along the road full of "honey buckets," which farmers bought to sprinkle the contents over their land. They called it "night soil," and it was responsible for our driving out to the studio each morning with the car windows firmly *up*. The U.S. Air Corps commemorated this little bit of Japanese custom by playing their annual service team's football classic in a stadium they renamed the Honey Bucket Bowl and by presenting an actual honey bucket to the winner.

Unfortunately, working together in Japan intensified and aggravated the differences Ray and I were experiencing in our relationship.

His direction carried over from reel life to real life. The phrase "male chauvinist" had not yet been coined, but it fit. I admitted I was hypersensitive, but he was hypercritical. Intuitively, I knew he felt I wasn't good enough for him.

I didn't measure up to his standard of perfection. Nevertheless, we stayed together and ignored the storm warnings.

When Ray's father, John Stahl, died in January of 1950, his mother moved to New York. We were in and out of the city frequently on business, and one weekend Ray suggested that we get married there almost immediately. I was stunned—unprepared emotionally and every other way. But I agreed.

I knew that it wouldn't be easy and that I would never be number one with him. That position was held by "Pums," Ray's mother, until the day she died. But like many brides, I thought that marriage might change him—that all differences would disappear with the "I do's."

We were married at the Little Church Around the Corner on March 31, 1951, and honeymooned in Bermuda. All arrangements were planned and taken care of by Pums. We moved in with her in her beautiful home on East 64th Street and became instant upper-crust New Yorkers.

We lived high, thanks to Pums. We traveled by limousine, dined each night with her at "21," the Colony, Quo Vadis, the Oak Room of the Plaza, or Gogi's La Rue. We saw every show in town with her, and they were fabulous. It was Broadway's golden age: *Pal Joey, Guys and Dolls, Judy at the Palace, The King and I, The Fourposter, Call Me Madam,* Olivier and Leigh in *Antony and Cleopatra.* Pums took me to lunch and Sophie fashion showings at the Waldorf, paid for beauty treatments at Elizabeth Arden's, for matinees, and for weekends in the country.

Having always been independent, I was uncomfortable being indebted to Ray's mother for everything. One morning, instead of sleeping until noon, I walked over to the

Conover Modeling Agency and signed with Harry and Candy Jones under the name Martha Lou Spring. On interviews, I left a card saying "Spring was here" and soon had appointments—every half hour of every day at twenty dollars an hour. I did a Philco ad, one for Noxema, mostly catalogue work.

Modeling was hard work—not glamorous at all—actually a bore. I longed to be involved in something that embraced the inner me, not just the outer. I was living the kind of life every woman dreams of, but spiritually I was lonely, a void waiting to be filled. I hungered for meaning in my life. It was in Africa that I began to find it.

Ray and George's next picture was *The Scarlet Spear,* made for United Artists in Kenya, British East Africa. My experience there remains seared into my soul.

There is an old saying: "He who drinks of the waters of the Nile will never be happy until he returns to drink again." It's true. Even today I feel the pull. Africa is like no other place in the world—the cradle of civilization. I was humbled by its vastness, its splendor.

We flew first to London, then on to Nairobi via Rome, Cairo, Aden, Saudi Arabia, and Ethiopia. Our film cast and crew stayed in cottages at Brackenhurst in Limuru, ten miles out of Nairobi. It was a country club with a golf course, tennis courts, bougainvillea-shaded cottages surrounded by mist-shrouded mountains. Heaven.

Nairobi was continental and charming—the Paris of East Africa. We were wined and dined at the New Stanley and Norfolk hotels, outfitted for safari clothes at Jimmy Ahmed's, and entertained beautifully by our East Indian friends. (The British imported cheap labor from India to help build the railroads across East Africa. When the job was finished, many Indians stayed on to become the backbone of the country's economy. At the time we were there, the ruling class was British, the merchant class East Indian, and the lower class the native Africans.)

We made a point of driving from Nairobi to Limuru single file with windows and doors locked because of the Mau Mau uprising. A state of emergency had been declared. We had to pass through Kikuyu territory to get to Brackenhurst, and *escaris* (native police) were stationed along the road to protect motorists at Banana Hill, a known Mau Mau hideout. All of our group carried guns for protection.

The *Mogambo* safari from MGM was going out into the bush at the same time we were but on a much larger scale. There was so much film activity, we called it Nairobi and Vine and wondered if Africa had "gone Hollywood." I often saw Grace Kelly and Clark Gable dining by candlelight in the New Stanley Grill. Eyelocks and stolen kisses indicated more was going on than what was in the script.

It looked as if Hollywood were turning the Dark Continent into a vast motion picture set. Trucks full of arc lights and reflectors lined the streets, and natives boasted proudly among themselves "Me MGM," or "Me UA." The lounge of the New Stanley Hotel was as full of trade gossip and rumors as any studio commissary.

It was the success of the films *King Solomon's Mines, The Snows of Kilimanjaro, Where No Vultures Fly,* and *The African Queen* that triggered this full-scale invasion. Nairobi became a boomtown. Safari equipment was at a premium, as were professional hunters, safari boys, carpenters, electricians, and construction engineers. Worried-looking American executives filled the cable offices and bars. Signs like B-S Ville, Africa and Little Hollywood were posted. Sari-clad autograph seekers (with red caste marks on their foreheads) waited endlessly in front of the New Stanley Hotel for a glimpse of the famous.

The MGM *Mogambo* safari will long be remembered by an awed Africa. In size, expense, and scope, it was monumental. It consisted of 150 vehicles and 150 people, and its accommodations rivaled those of a first-rate resort hotel. The stars of the picture had a clause in their contracts limiting them to flights on nothing smaller than a DC-3, so landing strips were built near thirteen jungle location sites to handle that size plane. Smaller planes flew in daily from Nairobi with fresh vegetables and filtered water. The unit "roughed it" in carpeted prefabricated houses, and for entertainment, movies were shown nightly (MGM having set up its own film exchange to book the pictures). A guide was assigned to each group of six people, and they had their own mess tent and cook. If a member of any group got bored and wanted a change of faces, he or she had only to refer the matter to the director of personal relations, and she saw to it that the person was transferred to a more congenial circle.

Classes were held to teach the natives to wear shoes and use the latrines in an effort to limit flies around the camp. A regular commercial radio station was set up so that Culver City, California, and darkest Africa were never more than a radio signal apart. Fleets of trucks traveled back and forth to Nairobi daily, and dieticians and cooks slaved tirelessly to appeal to temperamental MGM palates. No effort was spared to see to it that the inhabitants of Metroville remained one big, happy family. The company was bothered by rains, but

Nairobians felt certain the setback would be only temporary, as not even Mother Nature would dare defy the authority or production schedule of MGM in British East Africa.

We predicted that full-length mirrors and casting couches would probably become standard safari equipment. Natives who knew no other English would soon be able to understand "Quiet on the set," and SAG representatives would lurk behind thorn trees making sure no animal worked without a guild card. Africa spoke, but, at that time, Hollywood was writing the dialogue.

Ours was a minisafari, better in every way. When the short rains stopped, we started out one morning before dawn.

I'd heard that Kenya could mean the very poetry of life to those who responded to its splendor. Sunrise over the Great Rift Valley moved me to tears. From the escarpment, we could see huge herds of game dotting the open, rolling grasslands—zebras, kongoni, Thompson's gazelles, eland, topis, impalas, wildebeest, giraffes.

We made permanent camp deep in Masai territory under tall trees on the banks of the Mara River. There were eight tents around a central mess tent, a bonfire, and the radio shack, four hunters, ten of us, and twenty-six safari natives.

I was in a perpetual state of excitement. Safari never lost its fascination for me. The anticipation of the unexpected was thrilling—getting up in the morning never knowing what the day would bring. It could be the sight of a pride of lions on a kill, an elephant's charge, or rhinos attacking our trucks. It was the same excitement I felt as a child about almost everything, but there are few thrills like it for an adult.

I remember riding through the bush in the snake car with thirty puff adders, two cobras, and two pythons in the backseat. Our herpetologist promised to stop the truck to let me take pictures of anything interesting if I would help him capture snakes we saw on the path!

We took malaria pills, stored clothes in tin trunks, bathed in canvas tubs in heated river water, and quickly learned bladder control rather than get up in the night to walk to the outhouse on a path lined with gleaming animal eyes. I'll never forget the noises of the African night—the rasping cough of a lion, the laugh of a hyena, the bark of the baboon.

At Christmas, I decorated the tents with greens and paper stars. I cut out white paper Santa snowprints and placed them around the camp. The next morning, a leopard's prints were prominent alongside.

We made our bald cameraman a topi toupee for his birthday, along with an elephant dung cake. An elephant turd is shaped like a layer cake, so we iced it with chocolate, put candles on it, and gave Jim a birthday he'll never forget.

Safari food was delicious. My favorite was gazelle steak—seasoned and roasted, it tasted just like prime beef. We had fish from the river, tinned asparagus or sardines on toast, tinned butter and cheese, Jell-O, canned fruit. Everything was baked on an open fire. Breakfast was usually fresh pineapple, bacon and eggs, coffee, and toast.

I was a Technicolor redhead at the time, and Irene, George Breakston's wife, helped me keep it that way with touch-ups every two weeks. The transformation took place in the open air on the riverbank, and natives from miles around came to watch the bleaching and coloring and yell "Mimi engini," meaning "Me, next" in Swahili.

I decorated our tent overlooking the Mara River in "early African" with two Thompson's gazelle skins as rugs, a pair of topi horns mounted on the main tent pole, and guinea fowl feathers around my mirror.

One night a black cobra reared up between George's and Irene's cots. He couldn't shoot it because it was poised to strike directly in line with Irene's face. He called for help. One of the hunters appeared and shot it in the spine and killed it. The next morning, he held the snake by the tail at arm's length over his head, but he couldn't raise the other end off the ground. The cobra measured seven-and-a-half feet!

The Masai tribe worked with us on the film. They are cattle raisers, blood drinkers. They insert a tube in the neck of a living animal and drink its warm blood. The animal goes on living. They are Nilotic, and their warriors are the most beautifully built men in Africa. They live in filth in mud igloos with floors of cow dung as squishy as mud. Their warriors have a graceful, loping stride, are painted with ocher, are known for their bravery, and live by the code, "He who goes forward into battle may die. He who retreats *will* die."

The day I did my snake scene in the picture, Jezebel, the tame python, was shedding. A wild snake was substituted with its mouth taped together. The terrified expression on my face was not acting.

I'll never forget being inside Ngorongoro Crater—a miniature Africa; the Serengeti Plains; Kilimanjaro, with snow like melting vanilla ice cream dripping down its cone; the blue mass of the Ruwenzori Mountains. In the face of such beauty, there can be no question at all as to whether there is a power greater than ourselves directing it.

Hemingway was right when he wrote that Africa brings out the best or the worst in a person. In that mystical land, one comes face-to-face with oneself—like it or not. I affirmed life in Africa. I heard the song of the universe and realized the wonder and sheer beauty of existence. It was a spiritual experience. Never had I felt more keenly the presence of God.

And everything came into perspective for Ray and me there. We realized the problems with our marriage were never going to be resolved. Neither of us was happy.

Most nights, as I lay on my cot looking up through star-studded mosquito netting at the African supersky, Ray was in the radio tent trying to reach his mother in New York. The radio signal "V Q 4 N Z K—V Q 4 N Z K" became a litany, the epitaph for our marriage. It was clear that nobody would ever be as important to Ray as Pums, and I knew I could never be satisfied with second place.

There were other problems, too. It wasn't just my marriage I analyzed on those lonely moonlit nights. I took a good long look at me. I searched my soul. What did I want? Who was I? Where was I going?

I admitted my imperfections. I was an overachiever. I recognized that my ambition and my drive were not endearing qualities, but they were a part of me—and I'd never hurt anyone getting what I wanted. I never would.

I faced the fact that I had probably married Ray's mother, not him. She was such a strong-willed personality that I was thrilled to be accepted by her as good enough for her son. His former girlfriends had been tried and found lacking. I was the only one of whom she approved. Ray told me it was her decision that we should be married that prompted his proposal. He wrote: "I adore and admire Pums far above anyone in this world whom I've ever known or expect to know and I will do anything to make her happy." It was her life-style we enjoyed, her friends, her position, her financial backing. We were living a secondhand sort of life that did not engender respect or leave either of us with much dignity. I wanted more from a relationship, from life itself.

These sentences from a letter to me sum up Ray's feelings:

> I hope now you have had from me the frankness you have always wanted, that you understand a lot of things: Why, for example, I refused to give in to your pleas for children. It's relatively simple to readjust our own lives—and I knew someday we would have to. I have known it from the beginning. We should never have gotten married and probably never would have if Pums hadn't pushed it.

I left Ray in Africa, divorced him in California, made no financial demands. Sadly, he died very young of a malignant melanoma.

Looking back on my life with him, I realize we could never have been happy together. Our natures were too different—opposites, positive and negative.

Ray always expected the worst to happen. And so, to him, it always did. He never embraced life, never heard the music.

I lived on the bright side. No matter how many times I got knocked down, I came up smiling, believing that the championship was just a round away. Being born with a positive attitude is one of God's greatest blessings.

On a foggy day in 1953, I left Africa and flew home to California with no money and no prospects—little *but* that positive attitude. My life was at a very low ebb.

5

DREAMS COME TRUE

My agent had written me that Warner Bros. was doing a remake of Edna Ferber's *So Big* starring Jane Wyman. A search had been conducted for an actress to play the pivotal role of Paula, the society girl who battles for the affections of Jane Wyman's son. Fifteen girls had been tested—two had even been flown out from New York—but none of them seemed right. The picture started without the part having been cast.

As I stepped off the plane in Los Angeles, my agent, Louis Artigue, was there to meet me. He drove me straight over to Warner Bros. to meet with casting director Miles Gilbert. Miles took me down to the stage to introduce me to Jane Wyman, director Robert Wise, and producer Henry Blanke. I was given a scene from the picture to work on overnight and an appointment to read for them the next day.

At the appointed hour the next afternoon, I did the reading in Miss Wyman's portable dressing room on the set. When I finished, there was silence; then Wise said, "That's it, everyone. She's Paula." Just like in the movies!

I couldn't believe it. A few days before, I'd been in darkest Africa, and now I was in a whirl of fittings, conferences, interviews with columnists Hedda Hopper and Louella Parsons, and still photographs in the gallery. Incredible.

Most of my scenes were shot in the huge soundstages at Warner Bros. in Burbank. I blossomed under Robert Wise's sensitive direction. I loved being back—being a part again of only-in-Hollywood professionalism. It was six weeks of pure joy, and it showed in my work.

At the closing-night set party for the cast and crew of *So Big,* Jane Wyman came across the stage to say, "Paula, I just want to tell you that I've seen all your scenes, and I think they're wonderful. Good luck to you. I really think you'll go far." Her words meant a great deal to me. I wrote them in my diary that night and never forgot her graciousness.

Because of my work in *So Big,* Warner cast me as the second lead with Doris Day in *Lucky Me*—a big-budgeted Technicolor musical with Robert Cummings and Phil Silvers, directed by Jack Donohue. I played a rich society girl who vied with Doris for Robert Cummings's attentions. At one point, I was pushed into a swimming pool fully clothed in a designer ball gown. (The wardrobe department made three identical dresses in case we didn't get it right the first time.)

Stunning Angie Dickinson had a one-line bit in the film. It was the first picture of her very successful career.

Doris was not feeling well during the filming of *Lucky Me* but never showed it. She was always smiling and had the rare quality of making people feel good just by being near her.

Clockwise from top right: My mother and father—superparents; Forth Worth, Texas—cowgirl—age six; at age twelve I dreamed of becoming an actress

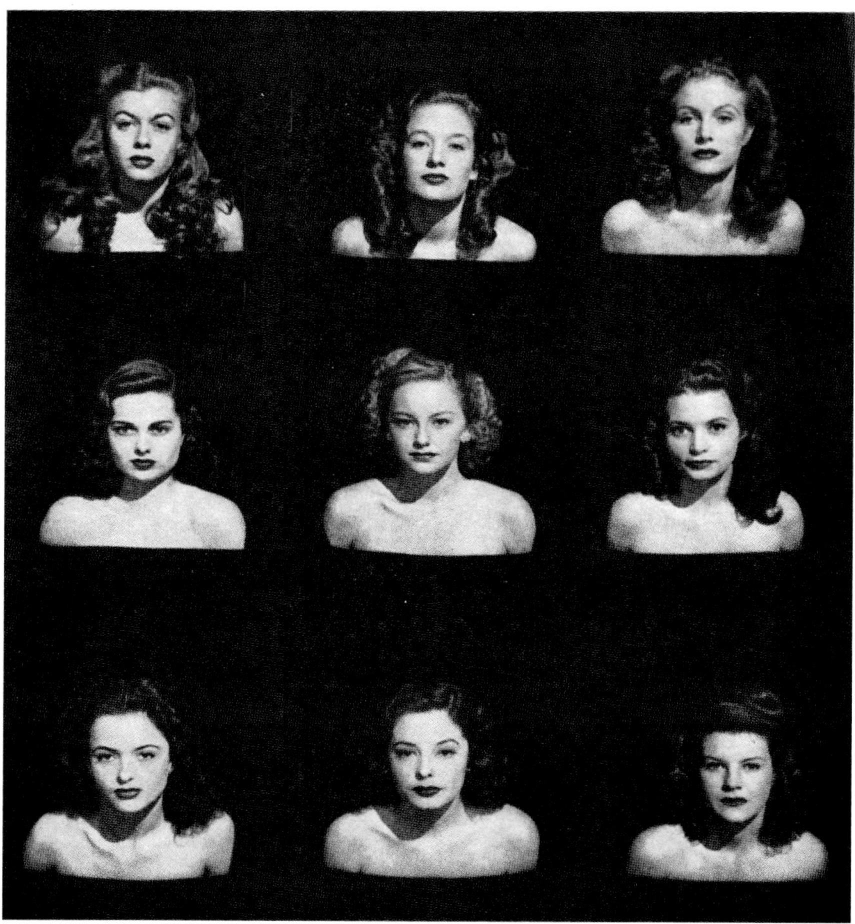

NANCY SAUNDERS, DEBRA ALDEN, VIRGINIA HUSTON (TOP); MARTHA HYER, MIMI BERRY, BONNIE BLAIR (MIDDLE); VONNE LESTER, JANE GREER, NAN LESLIE

Life Visits Nine Hopeful Starlets

Pretty young girls work hard at RKO and wait for the long chance which may make them movie stars

The nine girls on this page are all movie starlets whom the RKO studio is paying and training in the hope it may find one of them to be a new and different version of Katharine Hepburn or Ginger Rogers. Each girl is on a seven-year contract starting at $100 a week, but the studio may terminate the contract every six months.

A starlet leads a life of work and worry—the dedicated and ordered sort of existence enforced on officer candidates in the Army. Usually she knows little about acting and therefore must be instructed. Grooming and posture must be improved. Diction must be changed to remove all trace of local accent.

All the while, she worries about getting her contract renewed and about getting publicity. Even more than by schooling she helps herself by getting her picture in newspapers when she is chosen "Miss Poppyseed Roll" by the bakers association or "The Girl We Would Most Like to Tie Up To" by the dockers union. Finally comes a real screen test and then, in most cases, the ax.

RKO would be well pleased if just one of these nine starlets were to achieve stardom; the average at that studio has been one in 75. Best bets in the group seem to be Jane Greer, the former wife of Rudy Vallee, and Virginia Huston (*see p. 129*).

The hopeful starlet, *Life* magazine, February 18, 1946

Clockwise from top: *The Velvet Touch*, 1948, starring Rosalind Russell and Claire Trevor, was my first featured part in an important film; at RKO I became a star of the still gallery—always eager and available for photographic opportunities; the high school graduation picture that made my dream come true—by way of Germany.

Top: On location in Tokyo for *Geisha Girl*, 1952

The Stahls on safari in Africa for *The Scarlet Spear*, 1953; smiling with a python around my neck was the best acting I did in this film

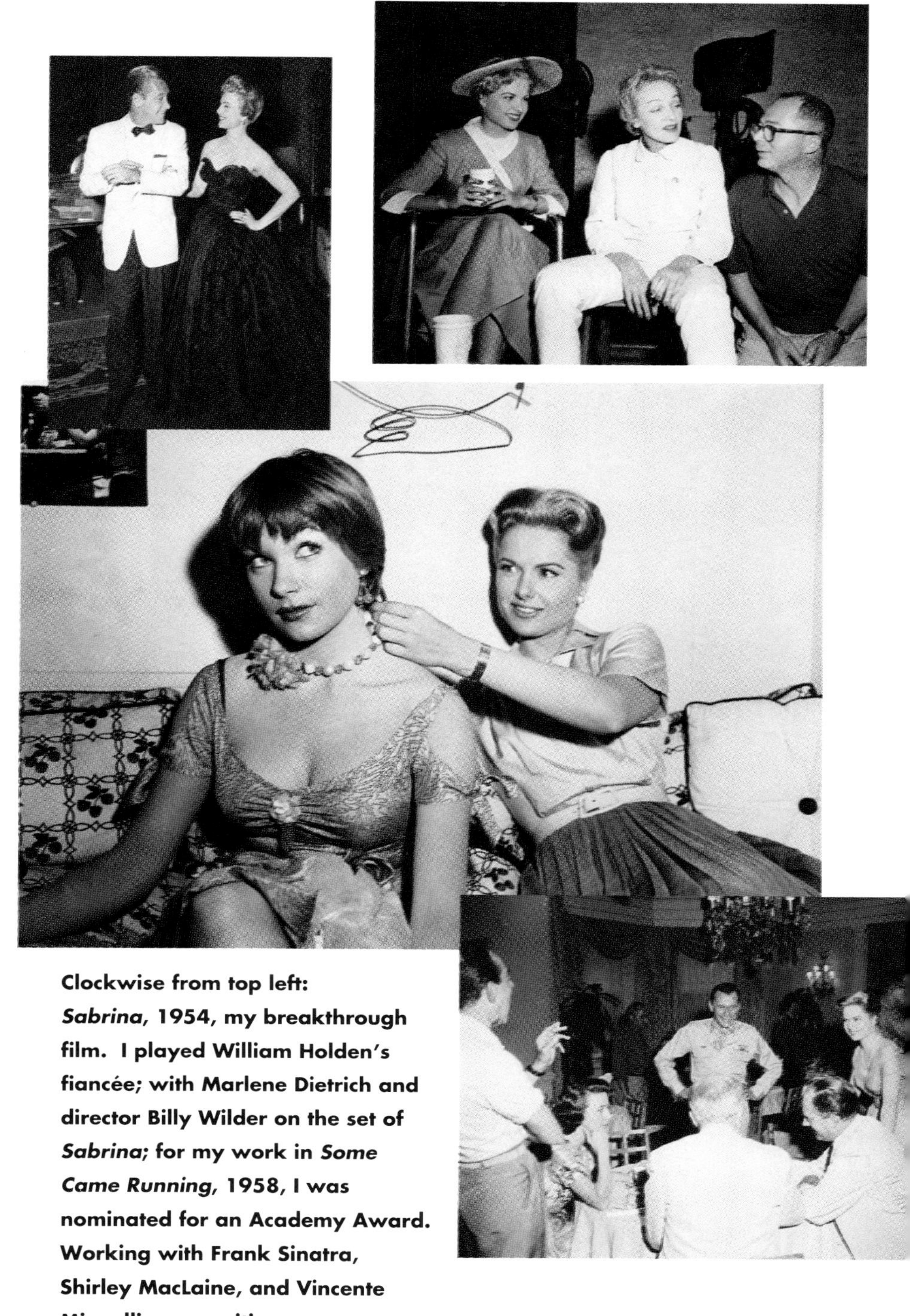

Clockwise from top left: *Sabrina*, 1954, my breakthrough film. I played William Holden's fiancée; with Marlene Dietrich and director Billy Wilder on the set of *Sabrina*; for my work in *Some Came Running*, 1958, I was nominated for an Academy Award. Working with Frank Sinatra, Shirley MacLaine, and Vincente Minnelli was exciting.

Glamour portraits

Leading men (from top):

Cary Grant, *Houseboat*, 1958
Frank Sinatra, *Some Came Running*, 1958
Tony Curtis, *Mister Cory*, 1957

Leading men (from top):

Marlon Brando, *The Chase*, 1966

Danny Kaye, *The Man from the Diner's Club*, 1953

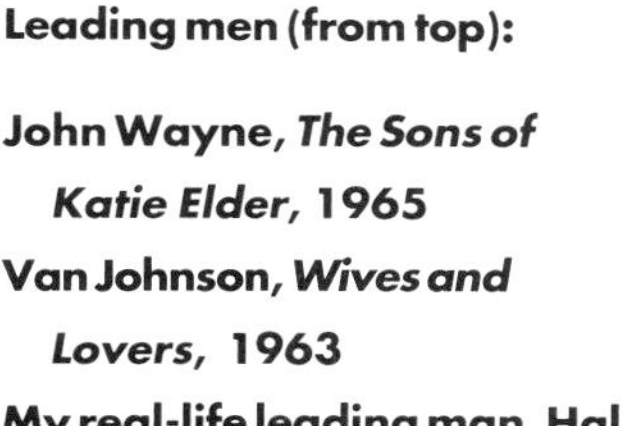

Leading men (from top):

John Wayne, *The Sons of Katie Elder*, 1965

Van Johnson, *Wives and Lovers*, 1963

My real-life leading man, Hal Wallis

The elements of elegance

In her Hollywood home, standing next to a Pissarro painting, Martha Hyer pours tea from a cherished Sheffield service. She says, "I love the gleam and grace of old silver. It is so proud and polished that I feel rich and queenly, drunk with its beauty."

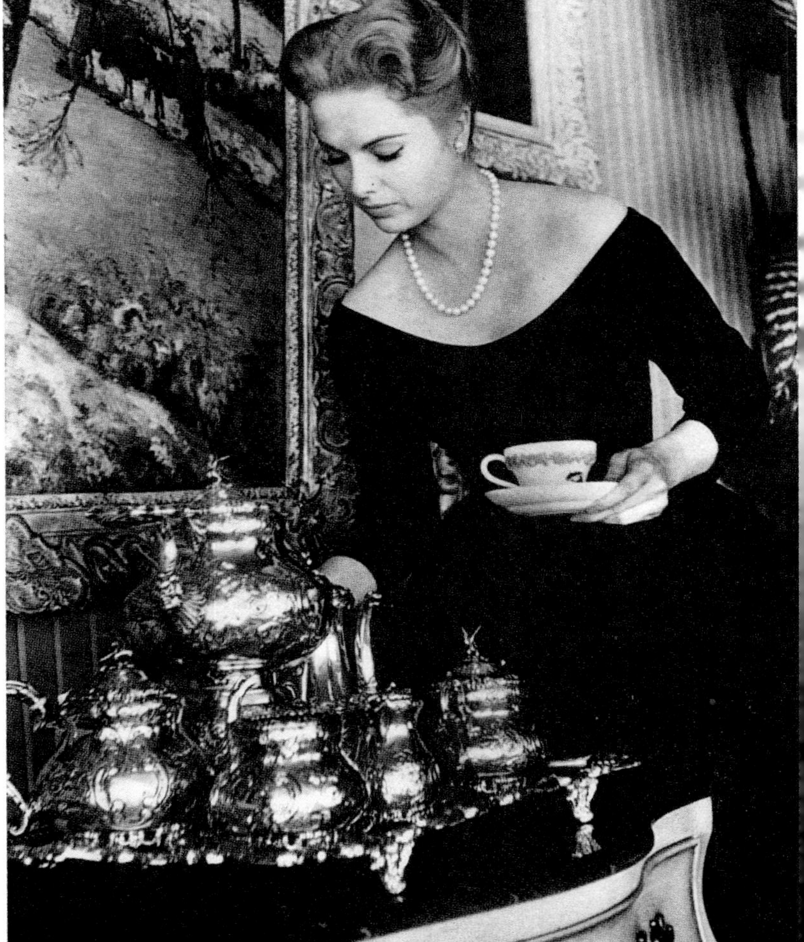

What most women want, Martha Hyer has

NOTHING BUT THE BEST

Martha Hyer, a beautiful woman of Hollywood, leads the life that, in whole or in part, many Americans would like to live—a life of independence and elegant luxury. She loves, openly and single-mindedly, only the nicest, most lusciously expensive things. She takes unabashed delight in the luster of old silver, the pampering warmth of fine furs, the colors of great paintings, the subtle flavors of vintage wines.

Happily for Martha Hyer, she can afford the things she covets. She is a success in a lucrative profession—movie acting—and she has worked hard doing leads in westerns, second leads in bigger films. This year she received an Academy nomination for her supporting role as the chilly schoolteacher in *Some Came Running*. She earns $100,000 or so a year and uses it to create a satisfyingly luxurious setting for herself.

This was not always so. Martha grew up in a middle-class home in Fort Worth, Texas amid the warm love of a passel of parents and sisters and often she goes running back to them. She spent long lean years in acting school and bit roles, later, briefly, tried marriage. Now a bachelor girl, she keeps elegantly aloof from the movie capital's usual entanglements. She is 30 now—likeable, intelligent and clear-eyed about what she is doing with her life. "If this is transitory," she says, "that is fine. I've dreamed a dream and it has come true. I am happy."

Photographed for LIFE by LEONARD McCOMBE

CONTINUED

Opposite: *Life* magazine, May 4, 1959

Meeting the Queen at the Royal Performance of Hal's *Anne of the Thousand Days*, 1969

From top:

Santa Fe, 1985

With Hal, Katharine Hepburn, and John Wayne on location for *Rooster Cogburn*, Bend, Oregon, 1975

Soon I was able to move from my tiny storeroom of an apartment into a charming country cottage in West Hollywood. No more standing in line for unemployment compensation. I was working constantly.

After finishing *Riders to the Stars* with Richard Carlson and Herbert Marshall, I did *Cry Vengeance* with Mark Stevens on location in Ketchikan, Alaska. Next came *Down Three Dark Streets* with Broderick Crawford, and lots of television, live and taped.

My big break came when I was cast as William Holden's fiancée in *Sabrina.* Billy Wilder directed. Audrey Hepburn, Humphrey Bogart, and Bill starred. I was lucky to have been even a small part of the picture. It was a classic.

Edith Head designed the clothes, and at Billy Wilder's suggestion, I became a blonde in contrast to Audrey Hepburn's dark hair. I liked being a blonde. It softened the shape of my large square face, instead of framing and accentuating it as dark hair did. I photographed better that way.

There was much friction, side-taking, and intrigue during the filming of *Sabrina.* Bill Holden was drinking heavily, and often, after a liquid lunch, had to rest until he sobered up.

One day, Bill was very shaky, blowing his lines and not really in shape to work. Bogie quietly remarked, "Methinks the lad hath partaken too much of the grape"—a barb that drove an even-deeper wedge into an already-deteriorating relationship.

Bill Holden reminded me of a cuddly Cheshire cat—his smile could charm the birds out of trees. I liked him very much. He was a good actor and a good person. All he lacked was discipline.

Bogart knew how important this film was to my career, and he helped me in every way he could. When we played scenes together, he made sure my face was photographed properly. He rehearsed with me, gave me helpful hints. That hard exterior hid a heart of gold.

When my sister Jeanne saw *Sabrina,* she said, "I can't believe that is *my* sister up there dancing with Humphrey Bogart." I couldn't either.

I had no scenes with Audrey Hepburn but found her to be a very special lady. This story shows her delicious sense of humor.

On the set of *Roman Holiday* (her first picture), the director William Wyler took her aside one day to explain that in films, pads were often used to make an actress look curvier, better endowed. He suggested she see the wardrobe people about it.

She looked up at him with those fabulous Hepburn eyes and whispered, "But, Mr. Wyler, I already have them on!"

In filming, there is more time spent off camera than on. Between scenes, as the technical crews "set up" a shot, the actors and actresses wait on the set in canvas chairs or in their dressing rooms, chatting, resting, or reading. When Marlene Dietrich visited her close friend Billy Wilder during the shooting of *Sabrina,* she often sat with me and shared her professional secrets. She analyzed my portrait photographs, pointed out mistakes in camera angles, advised me to wear classic hats and hairstyles that would not date my film appearances. She taught me how to accentuate my cheekbones and took me around to the back of the camera and made me look through the viewfinder to learn lighting techniques.

She seemed egoless—happiest when helping others. Over coffee and a piece of her homemade strudel one day, she reminisced about her tour of the army camps in Europe in World War II. She told me she always wore blue jeans and ate with the boys in their chow lines. When she performed, it was often on the back of a truck in an open field, illuminated by jeep headlights. She caught viral pneumonia working in the rain, but penicillin saved her life. One of her greatest memories was entering Rome in the triumphal Allied procession.

I'm convinced that Marlene Dietrich's beautiful spirit will be remembered even longer than her beautiful legs.

My social life after *Sabrina* was awesome. While I was working again at Warner Bros., Richard Gully came down on the set and introduced himself. He was social secretary to Mr. and Mrs. Jack Warner and invited me to a formal dinner party at their home for Pierre de Gaulle, a member of General Charles de Gaulle's family. My escort would be the French consul general accompanying the guest of honor and his date, Grace Kelly.

Thirty were invited to dinner and 150 to the supper dance after. I arranged with Paramount to borrow the black strapless Edith Head dress I wore in *Sabrina,* and my dinner partners, Gary Cooper and James Mason, were very complimentary. I was too excited to eat as I looked around the room and recognized John Wayne, Susan Hayward, Rex Harrison, Dean Martin, Alfred Hitchcock—just about every major talent in Hollywood.

The next day, Mrs. Gary Cooper called to invite me to a housewarming party at their new home in Bel Air, officially launching me into the stratosphere of Hollywood society. Rocky Cooper was a stunning-looking lady known for her great taste and elegance. Her parties were legendary.

Because of the kindness of hostesses like Rocky, Edie Goetz, Sylvia Kaye, Roz Russell Brisson, Anita May, Skip Hathaway, and Frances Goldwyn, I met and mingled with the most glamorous group of people in the world: the talented actors, producers, directors, and writers responsible for filmdom's golden age—Hollywood royalty.

Personally and professionally I prospered. I bought a beautiful home overlooking the city. When I told a friend that 1957 had been the best year of my life, she said, "But you said that last year and the year before."

I had boyfriends, lots of them. The only one I'll name was the one who meant the most—Gene Kelly. I'll always be his biggest fan, on-screen and off. The world remembers his "Singin' in the Rain." I'll never forget his kissin' in the rain.

The games we played then were so innocent compared with those of today. We had *romance*, fun. Ladies were wooed with champagne, caviar, gifts of jewelry, furs, property, and paintings. We were made to feel special. It was a time of dressing beautifully. We wore hose and heels, suits and gloves, hats, and lovely bags.

I loved my life. I was free, independent, a successful actress with a bright future. The excitement of mixing with, and being admired by, exceptional people was exhilarating. I wanted it never to end.

One night at a formal party at the Harry Cohns', I danced every dance with a new fan, a would-be beau. The next morning, a gift-wrapped black Thunderbird was parked in my driveway. Did I send it back? Would you?

On another balmy California night, I went to a dinner party at the Coldwater Canyon home of Jean Howard, ex-wife of agent-producer Charles Feldman. Over cocktails around the pool, I was introduced to a very handsome man. He was bright, charming, and articulate. We got along famously. He asked Jean to change the placement so that I would be seated next to him at dinner, and we continued our conversation and flirtation. Before he left, he scribbled his address and phone number on a cocktail napkin and urged me to lunch with him next day at the beach.

I didn't go. A lot of ladies did. The gentleman was Senator John F. Kennedy.

The greatest perk of my success was being able to share it with my parents. They saved this letter and I treasure it now.

March 17, 1956
Hollywood

Dearest Mom and Pop—

Tonight I'm able to do something I've wanted to do for a long while—something that gives me great pleasure and much happiness. Enclosed are checks for twenty-five hundred dollars for a trip to Europe for the two of you. It is money I never expected to get—my long promised deferment in "Scarlet Spear"—and I would rather do this with it than anything else in the world. Please don't tell me to save it. What good would the money be if I looked back years from now and remembered what I could have done for you and didn't?

I am so grateful to you both. I am the happiest I have ever been in my life—doing what I would rather do than anything—having only exciting things happening to me.

You were right, Mom—dreams do come true if you believe enough, work hard enough, and are lucky enough to have parents like you.

Have a wonderful time planning—and going!
I love you.

Your—
Marty

They sailed from New York on the *New Amsterdam.* Part of my gift was a park-side suite at the Plaza and house seats for *My Fair Lady.* I was working and couldn't be there to see them off—but no gift has ever given me, or them, greater pleasure.

When *Sabrina* premiered in Hollywood, I appeared in the black strapless Edith Head ball gown I wore in the film, with a stole made entirely of vanda orchids (courtesy of Paramount's publicity department). I was photographed and interviewed until I was exhausted, but it paid off. An executive from Universal Studios was there. He liked my performance in the picture, liked the way I was working at the premiere, and called my agent the next morning to talk a contract. He felt I could be their Grace Kelly. I signed with Universal and made ten films for them in three years.

My first picture was *Kiss of Fire* with Jack Palance and Barbara Rush, followed by *Red Sundown* with Rory Calhoun. In the former, I wore a long black wig, and in the latter I played a typically vacuous western heroine. This was Universal's Grace Kelly?

While I was playing a Wave officer opposite Donald O'Connor in *Francis in the Navy,* Dona Holloway came down from the front office to visit with me. She had been Harry Cohn's private secretary at Columbia for many years before accepting an executive position at Universal. She was the studio's direct connection to its contract players—our mother superior. Her job was to see that we were given every opportunity to be considered for a role before that part was given to an outsider. She was our troubleshooter. If teeth needed straightening, she interceded with the studio to advance the money. If weight needed to be lost, she set up reducing regimes. No problem was too large for her to tackle for us. Dona and I began a friendship that day that lasted thirty years.

(Dona married Lou Lichtenfield at our home in Palm Springs in 1967, and they became part of our family. Hal and I were heartsick when she died in 1984. I will never forget her loyalty, her devotion to her friends, her humor and dignity. She was Godsent to me and to all whose lives she touched.)

I made two pictures at Universal simultaneously: *Kelly and Me*, a Technicolor musical with Van Johnson and Piper Laurie, and *Battle Hymn* with Rock Hudson. I had only a few scenes in *Battle Hymn*, so the shooting schedules had been adjusted to enable me to do both roles. I would do scenes as the platinum-blonde movie star in *Kelly and Me* in the morning, then rush over to another stage in the afternoon to don a brown wig and play Rock's long-suffering wife. It got very schizophrenic but taught me I was truly a blonde now. I was uncomfortable in the dark wig. I didn't like the way I looked or felt as a brunette any more. (And I didn't enjoy working with Rock Hudson. He was a shallow little boy who may have grown tall but never grew up. Self-centered and spoiled, he could never communicate on any level that did not relate to himself.)

I was rewarded for this frenetic activity with the lead opposite Tony Curtis in *Mister Cory.* Written and directed by

Blake Edwards, it was a sleeper. We shot on location at Lake Arrowhead. Kathryn Grant (later Mrs. Bing Crosby) played my sister, and Charles Bickford an important character role. It was a very happy picture for all of us—a great showcase for contract talent.

I followed that with a role in Ross Hunter's remake of *My Man Godfrey* with June Allyson and David Niven. Again, the experience was delightful, largely because of David. He was witty, sophisticated, sensitive, and kind. I have never met anyone who didn't like David Niven.

The same certainly cannot be said of Jerry Lewis. Paramount borrowed me from Universal for the lead opposite him in *The Delicate Delinquent*, his first picture without Dean Martin. Jerry directed the film. It was *wild*—but good exposure and good experience.

I have always tried to keep my personal life private, a very hard thing to do in Hollywood. Newspaper columnists telephoned constantly for news items and gossip.

To appease Mike Connally of the *Hollywood Reporter*, I made up a beau—a doctor in San Francisco. Mike knew what I was up to but printed items in his column like "Martha Hyer off to San Francisco this weekend to attend the opening of the opera with her doctor friend there. It looks serious," or "You should see the diamond pin Martha Hyer's doctor 'friend' in San Francisco gave her for Christmas."

This fictitious affair went on for so long that I felt I had to end it some way, or marry the man. One morning, I looked at the headlines in the paper and telephoned Mike. In pseudotragic tones I cried, "Oh, Mike, my doctor was a casualty of the *Andrea Doria* disaster. He went down with the ship."

Connally burst out laughing—but he printed the item!

Paris Holiday with Bob Hope was a milestone in my career. I had read in the trade papers that the picture was to be filmed in Paris and that Bob's company was looking for a Grace Kelly-type to play the lead opposite him. Anita Ekberg had been cast in the other female role opposite Fernandel.

The part I had played in *My Man Godfrey* was similar to the role I wanted in the Hope picture, so Dona sweet-talked director Henry Koster into letting her take a reel of uncut film to show Bob in his private projection room. He liked me. Director Gerd Oswald liked me. I got the job.

The studio made money on the loan-out, so as a bonus, they gifted me with the mink coat I wore in *Godfrey.* All this and Paris, too!

It was my first trip to Paris, and I was dazzled. My wardrobe was done by Balmain, and I stayed at the Raphael Hotel. Everything was first-class.

In *Paris Holiday,* I played a State Department translator for Bob Hope and Fernandel. My French had to be perfect. I had studied it in high school, but I took a refresher course before the picture started. The crew spoke nothing but French, and I got so used to it, I even dreamed in French. One day a taxi driver asked me if I were Russian. He said I spoke French with a Russian accent, which pleased me. If he'd said with a Texas accent, I wouldn't have tipped him so generously.

Working with Bob was more like fun than work. He's a national treasure—a man of whom the entertainment world can always be proud.

Bob gave parties at Maxim's and Elephant Blanc. Francis Winnikus of United Artists took me to lunch at the famed Coq Hardi in the country, to candlelit dinners on the

Bateaux Mouches, to the Lido, to the Tour d'Argent, to the Louvre, to the world premiere of *Jeanne d'Arc* at the Paris Opera House, and Preminger's party at Maxim's afterward.

Easter weekend I flew to the Côte d'Azur and stayed in Cap Ferrat in the beautiful villa where *To Catch a Thief* was shot. I shopped, went to the gala in Monte Carlo, lunched at Eze Village, and dined in fine restaurants in Villefranche and Nice. *La vie en rose.*

But I longed for the right man I hadn't yet met. I stood alone on a balcony overlooking the moonlit Mediterranean one magic night imagining what he'd be like. Did it ever come in one package—love, respect, adventure, security, fun? One man? Would I go through life never finding him?

I hadn't met Hal yet, but I was looking for him.

When *Paris Holiday* was finished, I flew home by way of New York. It was an overnight flight and exhausting. I didn't pay much attention to my customs declaration. I should have.

The wardrobe I'd worn in the film had been given to me along with all the accessories—French bags, gloves, hats, and shoes. Baby Martha did not realize that gifts had to be declared and duty paid on them the same as on purchases. I hadn't listed any of it.

My luggage was confiscated at the airport, and I was sent to the ladies' room with an inspector who strip-searched me—a truly humiliating experience.

Lawyers appeared in court for me and paid the duty and a huge fine (the entire salary of my next picture). They told me that the customs agent who'd searched me said, "Oh, she was very cool about it. It didn't seem to bother her." (She didn't know I'd thrown up all the way into New York.)

When I got back to Hollywood, I was borrowed by Paramount for *Houseboat* with Cary Grant and Sophia Loren. Everything about that picture was exciting—the script, the clothes by Edith Head, the direction of Mel Shavelson, and particularly the off-camera love story that had us all agog. Cary was completely smitten with Sophia and was driving her crazy—along with everyone else—trying to get her to marry him. One day I picked up the phone in my dressing room and got a line crossed with theirs. He was pleading with her to marry him, promising her a trip around the world on a tramp steamer, the children she'd always wanted, anything, everything. I wanted to interrupt and shout, "If she won't, I will." Sophia listened very quietly, said little—and two weeks later was married by proxy to Carlo Ponti in Mexico.

Cary Grant oversaw all aspects of a production. If a set was dressed wrong, he'd often bring his own paintings or furniture to upgrade it. By this point in his long career, he had earned the right to approve wardrobe, script, casting, locations, just about everything involved in the films he made.

He was wonderful to me on *Houseboat*. When Sophia was unavailable, he often sat with me in my portable dressing room discussing philosophy, diet secrets, hypnosis, and people. Cary was very fond of Grace Kelly, and I was flattered when he said I reminded him of her. He admired a small diamond clip I wore so much that he had it copied—to give to Sophia? He took me for rides around the lot in his new Rolls Royce. He couldn't have been nicer.

Working in scenes with him was a joy. He was such a professional, and his timing was perfect. He was so good that he made everyone working with him look good, too.

I never brought up the fact that in 1948 I had done the soap commercial on a Lux Radio Theater show he'd starred in with Jeanne Crain. He'd probably have given me that great Grant grin and chuckled, "You've come a long way, baby."

Life magazine did a ten-page photographic layout in its May 4, 1959, issue: "What most women want, Martha Hyer has—Nothing But the Best." It documented my love of paintings, antiques, beautiful things, gracious living. It was newsworthy because that kind of life-style was unusual in Hollywood at the time. The kitchen-sink school of actors had taken over—torn T-shirts and jeans the uniform, motorcycles de rigueur.

Leonard McCombe shot the pictures, and to help with copy, I was asked by the editors to respond in writing to a list of subjects they'd sent me. They wanted my thoughts and very personal feelings concerning aspects of my life.

Here are those revealing notes written for *Life* in 1959:

> *On being alone.* I have to be, want to be, need to be—to be me. Maybe I'm too self-sufficient but I give so much of myself away in my work, I welcome the time when I can restore that energy—build up the inner strength that comes from quiet contemplation. When I get a free day or night to read or listen to music and just look at my view I feel as if I've been given a gift.
>
> *On determination.* Knowing exactly what you want is half the battle in winning it. My mother says that from the time I was born I wanted to do things

by myself. I never wanted help in putting on my shoes or clothes. I don't know if my determined jaw made a difference but it's there all right. One thing I've tried to do all my life is never let my ambition show. Nothing is more obnoxious to me than an aggressive woman. What I've tried to have is determination with dignity. I've never purposely hurt or embarrassed anyone in my drive toward success—but I set a goal early and moved as steadfastly and unerringly toward it as I could—a straight line. Any actor or actress tends to be greatly occupied with self because that's what you're selling. But I think it is very important that it not show.

The price I had to pay for success. The price everyone has to pay—hard, hard work, blows to my ego, sacrificing pleasure for work, disproportionate preoccupation with self often interpreted as selfishness by those who don't understand singleness of purpose. Whatever price I had to pay, it was worth it.

On marriage. I realized early on that I could never make a man happy unless I was happy, too—and what would make me happy was success in my work. So I'm married to my career at the moment. So far the union has proved successful. I feel I have a greater chance now of making a happy marriage. Maturity, fulfillment, the release from the tensions of struggle for identification and recognition will make me a better wife—eventually.

On elegance. I've always liked anything marked by refinement, grace or symmetry. The simplicity of something—its appropriateness is very important to me. I feel an interest in art and in everything beautiful contributes to the highest of all arts—the art of living. When one is surrounded by beautiful things one acquires a sense of appreciation for life in general. In social contacts, in my work, in all phases of life, the elegant life-style I have at home is part of my security blanket. It helps give me poise and confidence. I believe true elegance in a person is unselfconsciousness. When it is affected or assumed it disappears. Elegance is dignity—the knowledge that you look well, are dressed correctly, can handle any situation. It is being relaxed—free from strain. A truly elegant person is inevitably an aesthete—a believer in the theory of the beautiful. The elegant life is living with a keen sense of beauty, exhibiting refined taste—which naturally includes comfort and suggests luxury. How did I develop refined tastes? By absorption, study, living, travel, listening.

On a typical day in my life. I come awake quickly in the morning. Each day for me is like having a present to open. What's in store? What will it bring? I leave a note in the kitchen the night before telling Cleotha what time I wish to be called and what I want for breakfast. She knocks on my door at the appointed hour and by the time I'm back from the bathroom, she has my chair-pillow on the bed, the shutters opened to the sun and the view from the Pacific to downtown Los Angeles. She puts the two phones on my bed—both private, one *very* private—and brings my tray set with fine china and crystal. I even use a Steuben glass in the bathroom. What do people save their *best* for? What glass do you use more than the one in the bathroom and why does it have to be plastic? Surrounding oneself with beautiful things makes eating and drinking and living even more of a pleasure. I eat breakfast, read the papers and make phone calls (the telephone is a very exciting instrument in my life because everything that happens to me comes through it—my agent calling about interviews or new jobs, friends calling to make dates, my family touching base). I never take the luxury of breakfast in bed for granted. Most mornings I have to get up in the dark, drive to the studio, be in make-up for an hour, hairdressing for an hour, eat breakfast on the run, get into wardrobe and be on the set to begin shooting at eight o'clock. I work all day—even do interviews on my lunch hour—then drive home after dark at night, bathe, learn lines for the next day's scenes and try to be in bed by ten o'clock. This is my schedule every working day on a film. Breakfast-in-bed days are rare—and that's why I treasure them. Those days I never get out "on the wrong side of the bed."

On clothes. I love beautiful clothes and would rather pay more for a few really lovely gowns than have many inexpensive ones. I like basic classic clothes. Sometimes I go wild and buy a few crazy things but I recognize them as such. I try never to let a dress overpower me. Women may appreciate extremes in high fashion but men don't. They prefer a more conventional look. I also have to consider what will photograph well and whether someone else at an event might be wearing the same thing. When I fit my clothes I am very patient—even sit and walk in the fitting room so adjustments can be made if necessary to accommodate those activities. It's a real relief now not to have to pretend anymore that I have an oversized bust. I suffered through that phase of my career with padded bras and push-ups. Now people accept me as normal sized with emphasis on my work rather than physical qualifications. I feel good clothes are a wise investment because of the confidence they give you. If you feel perfectly dressed you are poised and relaxed. Soft colors are best for me—beige, white, pastels. Black, too. My coloring is so delicate I have to dress to draw attention to the face rather than the gown.

On me. I'm well organized. I like to plan things—make lists. Sometimes I'm impulsive and leap before I look. When I do make mistakes I try to learn from them, never look back or brood about them. I may be impractical with money but not with my life. I believe you get what you give—and if you're negative, life will be, too. But if you expect good things and work and fight for them, they'll happen. My ultimate goal is to be recognized as a really fine actress and have a good, sound marriage. There's a very simple word that has been the *X* factor in my success—faith. Faith is believing and knowing in the face of great odds. We all know the power it has. All my dreams seem to be coming true. I try to live gratefully.

These words were written by a person I hardly recognize today. In 1959, I was fascinated by possessions and a luxurious life-style. Material wealth and fame seemed all-important.

When the story appeared in *Life*, friends warned me it was an open invitation to a robbery. It pictured my home, high on an isolated hill, my painting collection, my beautiful silver collection, my Lincoln Continental—all the trappings of material success. And it mentioned that I lived alone.

I pooh-poohed their warnings. I didn't even have a burglar alarm. In those days, few did.

One evening, I went to a lovely party at the home of Merle Oberon in Bel Air. When I returned very late, I noticed immediately that two of my Impressionist paintings—a Renoir and a white-period Utrillo—were gone, their frames empty and askew on the wall.

By the time the police got there, I had discovered that furs, jewelry, and cash had also been stolen. The drawers and closets in my bedroom had been ransacked. My personal life was laid bare, no longer personal. I was shattered.

The police, and later the FBI, told me they had been waiting for it. The *Life* article had practically guaranteed a break-in.

There were few clues, and the gossip that began circulating broke my heart. It revealed to me the dark side of human nature—the desire to believe the worst no matter what the truth. One story was that a married man had given me the paintings and that either he or his wife or both had arranged the robbery to get them back. The truth was that I had purchased the paintings on an installment plan from Dalzell Hatfield Galleries in Los Angeles. Ten percent of my paycheck every month went straight to the gallery to reduce the balance on my account there. Another story making the rounds was that I had arranged the robbery for the insurance money.

Nobody, absolutely nobody, wanted to know, or believe, the truth. The gossip columns were full of innuendos. People whispered and giggled when they saw me. It was so unfair. But it showed me who my real friends were.

The police, the FBI, and Interpol worked together on the case. Then the Los Angeles Police Department called one day to tell me an informer had spotted the paintings in downtown L.A. in the trunk of a car, and they were on their way to make an arrest. The next I heard was that the pictures had been taken over the border into Mexico.

Months passed, and nothing happened. I gave up hope that the jewelry would be recovered. I was told it had been fenced and broken up immediately after the robbery.

I flew to Bangkok and later to Munich to film *Mistress of the World.* Upon my return, the insurance company called to tell me that the thieves had been unable to dispose of the paintings because they were so well known—"hot" in the vernacular. They were willing to make a deal with the insurance company to return them for a fraction of their value.

So one rainy night—like an episode of "Hunter" or "Matlock"—my lawyer, myself, an insurance investigator, and Dalzell Hatfield (the art expert from whom I had purchased the paintings) met in my lawyer's office in Beverly Hills. As they had been instructed by phone, the insurance representative and Hatfield drove to meet the informant at Tom Bergin's Bar on Fairfax Avenue near Wilshire. They switched to his car, then traveled to a remote shack in the Crenshaw district, where they were shown the paintings. Hatfield authenticated them and confirmed that they were in good condition, rolled but undamaged.

Ransom money was exchanged for the paintings, and much later in the evening we celebrated their return with champagne and congratulations all around.

The insurance company had compensated me for the loss shortly after the robbery. Fortunately, there had been a clause in the policy that allowed me to buy the paintings back at that same price if they were recovered. They had increased in value considerably since the robbery.

6

AND THE WINNER IS...

When I first read James Jones's book *Some Came Running* in 1958, I felt instant empathy with the character of Gwen French. I longed to play her on the screen, but I knew my chances were slim.

I met James Jones when I was in New York to do a live television show, "The Best of Broadway." After rehearsal one night I went with a group of friends to Goldie's for a drink and a late supper. Sydney Chaplin introduced me to James Jones and his wife, and later we all went to the Joneses' apartment for a nightcap.

During the course of the evening, I told him how much I liked the book and how I yearned to play Gwen. He told me he thought I would be perfect casting but that he had nothing to do with it. MGM would be making the picture and the decisions. We both agreed that Deborah Kerr or Jean Simmons or Eleanor Parker would get the part.

A few months later, MGM announced that Frank Sinatra, Shirley MacLaine, and Dean Martin would star in *Some Came Running*, but the role of Gwen French had not yet been cast.

One night at a dinner party, I was seated next to Bert Allenberg, a very important agent. We talked of *Some Came Running*, and I wistfully mentioned my "impossible dream" of playing Gwen. He said maybe it wasn't so impossible after all. We made a handshake deal then and there for his office to represent me.

I had just parted professional company with my agent of many years, Louis Artigue. It's very sad to leave a small agent after he's worked with you and helped you, held your hand, done all of the suffering with you on the climb up the ladder. I had been loyal to Louis Artigue. I stayed with him far longer than I should have for many reasons. But Louis worked at the casting director level, whereas Allenberg of the William Morris office went straight to the top. He sold the script, the director, and the stars to the studio as a package.

He took me to meet Sol Siegel, the producer of the film. Just being at MGM was the realization of one of my dreams. I had always loved that studio's product, had grown up on their films. To work there was my idea of "making it"—like a vaudevillian playing the Palace.

Mr. Siegel and director Vincente Minnelli said they would run film from other pictures I'd done to see my work. No test would be necessary.

Mr. Allenberg decided it would be wise for me to leave Universal. My contract there had not expired, but the studio had just been sold and few pictures were being made. The agency advanced me the money to buy off my contract (it wasn't much), and I was free to go for the gold.

Mr. Siegel and Mr. Minnelli liked the film they saw, Mr. Allenberg, who handled Frank Sinatra, got his approval, and my dream came true. I played Gwen French in *Some Came Running.*

I don't fool myself—I got the role in *Some Came Running* because I was handled by a top agent with considerable clout. The William Morris office handled Jean Simmons, Deborah Kerr, and Eleanor Parker, and they all wanted the role. But Deborah Kerr was working; Allenberg convinced Jean Simmons that it wouldn't be good for her; and he put Eleanor Parker in another picture.

Every night as I saw the "rushes" (the uncut film scenes shot the day before), I realized how very special the picture was going to be. Shirley was brilliant, Frank never better, and Dean simply marvelous.

I believe Dean Martin could have won an Academy Award if he had changed his billing. Bama, the character he played, was perfect for him. He should have taken a billing cut and campaigned for a nomination as a supporting actor.

I loved working for Vincente Minnelli. His direction was personal, sensitive. He was a perfectionist and even suggested how the character might stand or move in a certain way. A lot of actors don't like that kind of direction. I do. He thought of the picture as a whole, and was closely involved in every creative aspect of it—script, wardrobe, hairstyling, set design. (Incidentally, the house in *Some Came Running* got more fan mail than the actors did. MGM sent plans of that beautiful farmhouse to people all over the world.)

Shirley MacLaine had been loaned to MGM for *Some Came Running* by Hal Wallis—she was under contract to him. Between scenes, we sat in our dressing rooms and talked, often about Hal. She was miserable being under contract to him and wanted her freedom. Shirley was marvelous in the picture. She received her first Academy nomination for it.

I'll never forget the day Frank and I were scheduled to do our biggest scene—the one in which he was to take down my hair. It was a very complicated scene, and Minnelli had worked it out down to the last detail.

Frank walked onto the set at 1:00 P.M. (he liked to work Continental hours—1:00 P.M. to 8:00 P.M.) and said he had hired a train to take a group of his friends to Las Vegas for Judy Garland's opening. He was leaving at three o'clock. We all gulped and said fine. That gave us two hours to do one of the most important scenes in the picture.

We rehearsed with Frank's stand-in, as Frank feels he loses spontaneity and naturalness in his performance if he rehearses.

Everything was finally ready technically. Frank was shown his moves and marks, and the cameras rolled. It was a very difficult shot, with the camera moving in and out so that the whole scene was done in one continuous take with no cuts.

We did it one time, perfectly. Frank smiled, clapped Minnelli on the back and said, "That's what you get when you work with pros, Vincente," and left to catch his train.

It was one of the most talked about scenes of the film. I think Frank Sinatra is a very underrated actor. It takes great ability to play a role so believably that the performance seems effortless.

The role of Gwen French was the first real character part I'd played. And the hardest. I consider everything I did before it preparation. I had always played myself. For that part, I became someone else.

Gwen was an interesting person—very uptight, very withdrawn. All the things that I had taught myself not to do on the screen, such as keeping my mouth rigid or seeming nervous or tense, I now did because that was what the character was all about—a very repressed lady in a small town. When Frank Sinatra takes the pins out of my hair and it all falls down, all of Gwen's inhibitions fall down, too. At rushes, I saw myself magnified hundreds of times on the screen, and it depressed me to see again all the things that I had worked to eliminate from my screen self. More than anything else, motion-picture acting is naturalness and looseness, not letting the work show.

I also hated the way I looked. As a frustrated small-town schoolteacher, I was dressed plainly, even severely. My hair was made to look drab and pulled back tightly into a bun, and I wore flat-heeled shoes and little or no makeup.

Actors can seldom evaluate their own work. By the time the picture was over, I was convinced I'd never get another job. I confided in a friend that I had never acted or looked worse in a picture. I actually sat down and listed the ways to go if I was finished in films. I could teach, work in advertising or merchandising, maybe write. I think I was so immersed in the role that it carried over into my own life. For a while, I became as insecure and neurotic as Gwen French.

I first heard I had been nominated for an Academy Award for my supporting performance in *Some Came Running* in Egypt. I was on a publicity junket to Cairo for the opening of the new Hilton Hotel. (The planeload of celebrities included Hedda Hopper, Art Buchwald, Leonard Lyons, Van and Evie Johnson, and dozens more.)

We were at the pyramids when a man came speeding across the desert with an "urgent" cable for Miss Hyer. It was from my press representative and friend, Richard Carter, and read, "Congratulations on your Academy nomination. Now they will all come running."

It was a press agent's dream, but true. Leonard Lyons said in his column that I got the news by "Camelgram."

The only campaigning I did was very dignified and low-key. I took out quarter-page ads in the trade papers that consisted of a still picture from the film and one-line excerpts from favorable magazine and newspaper reviews.

Jean Louis designed the dress I wore to the awards ceremony, and it was beautiful, beige *peau de soie* with a sweetheart neckline. The bodice was beaded with seed pearls and gold. It had a tight waist, three-quarter-length sleeves, and a full skirt. With it, I wore a single strand of pearls and pearl earrings. When we fitted the dress, the fitters teased me and made me hold a pair of scissors in my hands as an Oscar substitute. We wanted the sleeves to look right in that possible winning position!

The awards ceremony in 1959 was at the Pantages Theater in Hollywood, and my escort for the evening was actor-friend George Nader. I hired a chauffeur-driven limousine to take to the awards and to the Academy dinner party afterward at the Beverly Hilton Hotel.

When I walked into the lobby, an MGM executive came over and said, "The odds in Las Vegas are five-to-one that you will win it."

I was seated on the aisle (as all nominees are). David Niven, who was seated opposite me, leaned over and said, "You have it made. It's the only sure thing of the evening." I threw him a kiss, held up crossed fingers, and with a thudding heart thought, "Could it *really* happen?"

It didn't.

The nominees were announced:

Maureen Stapleton for *Lonelyhearts*;
Cara Williams for *The Defiant Ones*;
Peggy Cass for *Auntie Mame*;
Wendy Hiller for *Separate Tables*;
Martha Hyer for *Some Came Running*.

The envelope was opened, and the winner was—Wendy Hiller, for *Separate Tables.*

I tried to be a good loser. But when I got home, I cried all night. I didn't know the best was yet to come.

My next film was *Ice Palace* for Warner Bros. I liked the part I played and enjoyed acting with such pros as Richard Burton, Carolyn Jones, and Robert Ryan. It was a good film but could have been better if the chemistry between the two leading men had been more like the electricity Burton generated with the ladies on the set. He was as active behind the camera as in front of it.

To his pleas of "Now come on, darling—you're the only one who hasn't," I teased, "E pluribus unum is not my style, Richard—particularly with someone who kisses and tells."

Richard reminded me of a rascally puppy. If the government could have bottled and sold his charm, sex appeal, and talent, they'd easily have wiped out the deficit. But how he squandered it!

My role in *Desire in the Dust* at 20th Century Fox was the kind of part actresses dream of playing—a sensual, Southern vixen with no morals and no conscience. Raymond Burr and Joan Bennett were cast as my parents. We filmed it on plantations near Baton Rouge, Louisiana. It was a super little picture, the poor man's *Tobacco Road.*

In *The Last Time I Saw Archie* for United Artists, Robert Mitchum, Jack Webb, France Nuyen, and I reenacted Jack's and Bill Bower's World War II experiences. I played Jack's girl, and France played Mitchum's. In one scene, Bob held a kiss with France long after the director yelled cut. Jack said in a very loud voice, "There seems to be an awful lot of offstage kissing going on in this picture." Mitchum yelled back, " . . . and absolutely no fucking." There was a shocked silence as Bob looked up and realized that there were nuns on the set watching the shooting. I don't know if he was embarrassed—the rest of us certainly were. And more than a little angry when he did poster art in the still gallery with his fly open, intentionally. Every photo had to be killed and redone—another full day's work.

I remember three things about *The Man from the Diner's Club* for Columbia: first, Danny Kaye was a sweet, sensitive, moody guy—not funny offstage at all, maybe even a little sad; second, I got to wear a gorgeous white wedding dress with all the trimmings—something that never happened in real life; and third, I had to do a scene in an open helicopter, which taught me never to go near one again.

The Carpetbaggers for Paramount was *fun.* It was a good script from one of Harold Robbins's best books, and Joe Levine publicized it to the hilt. After playing so many cool, uptight society ladies, I loved being Jenny Denton, the whore with the heart of gold.

I thought George Peppard was very good, Carroll Baker, too, and Elizabeth Ashley was excellent. She and George fell in love during the picture as well as in the picture. They were later married. Elizabeth is very much like the character she played in the film. She's bigger than life—almost too much for the screen, great in a theater.

The Carpetbaggers was Alan Ladd's last picture. He had a drinking problem, and "friends" who should have known better slipped him drinks on the sly. Tragic. He was trying so hard to make a comeback.

Columbia's *First Men in the Moon* was science fiction and very well done. It was filmed at Shepperton Studios in London and starred Lionel Jeffries. The story line: a British-Russian-American spacecraft lands on the moon and finds evidence that someone else has already been there—an eccentric inventor and his daughter and a young journalist. Our adventures were shown in flashbacks.

The moon people—Selenites—were played by a group of very hip cockney street kids. The comments they made about their costumes (in that accent) were hilarious. Fortunately, they crept about silently in the film.

Another thing I remember about this picture is coming back to the Dorchester Hotel one evening after work and being told by the desk clerk that President Kennedy had been shot in Dallas. I was stunned—as the world was—and stayed glued to the television set all night. Several British friends called to predict that it was the beginning of World War III and that American bombers were probably en route to Moscow. I think they were amazed at the way our anguished country handled the tragedy.

In 1963, I was thirty-nine years old and working constantly. Other actresses envied my busy schedule. I still lived in my beautifully romantic hillside house but had little time to enjoy it. My life was a round of film location trips, quick visits with my family in Texas, and spa stays to keep in shape.

Any spiritual stirrings I'd felt were put on hold as I lived life in the fast lane—pursuing the wrong goals, chasing over the rainbow for that pot of gold I thought all-important.

I did thank God each night for my success, petitioned Him for more of the same, requested that He take good care of my family and me. Me, me, me. I didn't know then that the secret of prayer is "Thy will be done, not mine." I was still trying to make deals with God, telling Him what to do, wanting it done my way.

I shared my newly found affluence with family and friends, was known as a "good" person, but I had little time for introspection and none for spiritual growth. Life was a cabaret, a carousel I rode that spun faster and faster. Represented by the great Jack Gilardi, I made one picture after another.

A Girl Named Tamiko with Laurence Harvey and France Nuyen, directed by John Sturges, was not one of my favorite films. Nor was Laurence Harvey one of my favorite leading men. I found him very much like the sneering misfits he portrayed on the screen. Doing love scenes with him took all my acting ability and a strong stomach.

Wives and Lovers with Van Johnson, Janet Leigh, and Shelley Winters was a different story altogether. Directed by John Rich, the picture was a pleasure from the first day of shooting to the last.

Van Johnson's smile, his positive attitude, and his upbeat personality endear him to everyone he meets. He's a big marmalade pussycat—professional, fun, considerate. During the filming of *Wives and Lovers,* Van tested positive for a cancerous lymph node. He never talked about it, never complained, finished the picture on high, then had surgery. It was a success, and he has been working steadily ever since. I'm convinced his affirmative outlook and cheerful disposition contributed to his recovery.

Janet Leigh is another example of the goodness I found in Hollywood. She has had her share of triumph and tragedy (a suicide in her family, divorce, childhood illnesses), but she is always enthusiastic, kind to everyone, and a pleasure to work with. Just before a scene was to be shot, she'd go off by herself and quietly repeat a simple prayer: "Life is the showing forth of the very self of God." She said it helped set her head straight.

The Sons of Katie Elder with John Wayne and Dean Martin was shot in Durango, Mexico. Henry Hathaway directed. He was charming socially but miserable to work with, reducing strong men to tears on every picture he made.

After his lung cancer operation, Duke Wayne had aged and was sensitive about his looks. As his leading lady, I was deglamorized in the role of a country schoolmarm. I wore little makeup, old clothes, and plain hairstyles. Critics said, "What has happened to Martha Hyer? She's lost her looks." So much for authenticity.

Bikini Beach, Picture Mommy Dead, House of 1,000 Dolls, and several pictures I made in Europe are all ones I'd rather forget.

I enjoyed doing *The Happening.* It was made in Miami with Faye Dunaway and Anthony Quinn, directed by Elliot Silverstein. My favorite line in the picture was one I spoke to kidnappers demanding ransom for my husband (Quinn): "For a hundred thousand dollars, you can keep the son of a bitch."

Tony brings such strength and energy to a scene that working with him is like holding your own in a hurricane. He's a director at heart—likes to tell everyone what to do and how to do it—but if we only did it his way, we'd all be Anna Magnani clones.

Making *The Night of the Grizzly* with Clint Walker, directed by Joe Pevney, was another happy experience. It was shot on location in Arrowhead and has become a Disney-type favorite on television.

The Chase for Columbia was produced by Sam Spiegel, directed by Arthur Penn, and scripted by Lillian Hellman. The picture didn't really come off, but it was exciting to work with Marlon Brando, Robert Redford, Jane Fonda, Miriam Hopkins, Angie Dickinson, Robert Duvall, and Janice Rule.

Making *Mistress of the World* with Carlos Thompson was exciting. It was a German film shot on location in Bangkok and at Angkor Wat in Cambodia. I flew to Thailand by way of Hong Kong. At the Peninsula Hotel, I ran into Bill Holden—"Mr. Hong Kong"—who took me to dinner and showed me the best of that fascinating city.

When the plane door opened in Bangkok, I thought I'd walked into an oven. I stayed at the Oriental Hotel on the river and loved visiting the temples and the klongs (canals), tasting spicy Thai food, and shopping for Thai silk, antiques, and gemstones.

The Vietnam War was a few years in the future, but in Laos and Cambodia, fighting had already begun. Soldiers of fortune swarmed into Bangkok. Intrigue was rampant. Military types double-talked in hushed tones.

I rode to location on an elephant at Angkor Wat and enjoyed exploring every corner of that mysterious ancient temple overgrown with tangled vegetation. It was the palace of a vanished race, a lost civilization.

William Dieterle directed the picture. He was old and ailing but still commanded respect. Even in the jungle, he wore white gloves (his trademark) and never made a move unless his wife approved it astrologically.

Actors of every nationality appeared in the film, each speaking his own language. Later it was dubbed into the language of each country in which it was to be distributed and shown. At the premiere in Munich, we all spoke perfect German. When I saw the picture in France we spoke French. In Italy, Italian. I never saw it dubbed in English.

7

LIFE AT THE TOP

The most important thread woven into the tapestry of my life was Hal Wallis. I believe our relationship was ordained.

One sixties summer day, I flew to New York to publicize *The Big Fisherman,* a biblical film I had appeared in for Walt Disney Productions.

Standing in line at the airport, I met the stare of a very attractive man leaning against the counter. His magnetic blue eyes laserlocked mine. I recognized him—the legendary Hal Wallis, superproducer. We'd met before, but no lightning had struck then, no skyrockets had gone off, no bells had rung.

They did now.

On the plane, he sat in the seat behind me, and we got acquainted. Just before we got to New York, he asked me if I'd like a ride into the city and to have dinner with him that night. I told him I was sorry but someone was meeting me and I had a date for dinner. He asked me out for the next night, Sunday. I told him I was going to the country for the day. Then I waited for him to ask me out for Monday—and waited, and waited, and waited. Nothing happened. Finally, I leaned between the seats and said, "How about Monday?" And we made a date. He said later that if I hadn't persisted, we would never have gotten together. He thought he was being rejected, and he wasn't going to ask me again.

We became close.

I made many films on location during our "courtship." An incident occurred during one trip that makes me blush to remember even today.

I missed Hal very much and told him so in a heartfelt cablegram. It didn't embarrass me when I sent it from the Imperial Hotel in Tokyo. The embarrassment came later when Hal told me how he had received it.

He was having a production meeting in his office—lots of people seated around a conference table. When the studio operator buzzed that she had an urgent cable from the Orient, he asked her to read it, forgetting that he was on a speaker phone. So, for all to hear, she read, "My mouth wants your mouth, signed, Martha." After a pregnant pause, Hal smiled and said, "Isn't that nice. Will you get a copy and send it to my office please? Thank you"—and went right on with the meeting. I'm afraid our courtship wasn't so private after that.

Hal had another life and I had another life, but what became most important to both of us was our life together. We were good for each other, enjoyed the same things, never argued, never fought. We fit. His constant refrain was, "I wish I'd met you years ago."

We were married by a judge on December 31, 1966, in Palm Springs, California. Later we had another ceremony at Temple Israel in Los Angeles, with Rabbi Nussbaum officiating.

I'm certainly not the paragon Hal describes in his book *Starmaker*, written with Charles Higham, but it's wonderful to know that he felt I was.

> Martha is blessed with a good disposition and a quick, bright mind. No matter what happens, she handles it with strength and a smile. I feel relaxed with her. Always up—always happy—she sees the bright side of every situation and is a marvelous companion. She loves spectator sports as much as I do, enjoys travel, eats with gusto, and has an enthusiasm for life I find catching. Unselfish and generous in her efforts to please me, she never complains or acts possessive, never asks what I've done or where I've been. Her motto is "You hold the tightest with a loose hand."
>
> A gregarious person, Martha mixes freely and easily with people, is kind, sensitive, affectionate. We laugh a lot—she has a great sense of humor.
>
> During one evening in her beautiful hillside home, she surprised me with stone crab and key lime pie from Florida. We had spent many happy hours at Joe's Restaurant in Miami, so she telephoned and had them fly out my favorite dishes.
>
> One birthday she called my office, asking me to cancel all appointments and spend the day with her. When I arrived at her house, a chauffeur-driven limousine was waiting. Martha's birthday gift was

Disneyland—a complete set of tickets for every ride. We spent the day and evening like a couple of kids—enjoying the attractions, eating too much, just plain having fun.

We made wonderful trips to Taormina in Sicily, Bad Gastein in Austria, Capri, Venice, Mexico, Hawaii.

I'll never forget crossing to Naples on the Italian liner *Leonardo da Vinci*. It was a happy cruise but we were puzzled and made uncomfortable by people's stares. I wore black sweaters and slacks almost exclusively at the time, and Martha and I seldom mixed with others on board. We are very private when we travel, enjoy our own company, and always request a table for two. Just before we disembarked, a fellow passenger and friend of mine from Hillcrest Country Club in Los Angeles came over and said, "Hal, I didn't want to bother you, but people have been speculating about you two. They finally decided that you are a Mafia don deported to Italy and Martha is your blonde, young moll." We laughed about it but I stopped wearing all-black gangster garb immediately.

I was happier with Martha than I had been for many years.

Martha decided to give up her career when we married and says she has never regretted it. From the beginning, our marriage has been a happy one.

Martha moved from her lovely home into my house on Mapleton Drive. Her art collection and antique furniture blended perfectly with mine. She has a tremendous flair for decorating and I tease her that she redecorates after every film I make according to where we've been on location. After *Anne of the Thousand Days* and *Mary, Queen of Scots,* we went through our English period. After *Red Sky at Morning* and *True Grit,* we built a second home in Palm Springs to house our growing collection of Western Americana.

Architect Harold Levitt designed an informal, Santa-Fe-style ranch house for us. It is southwestern in feeling—adobe brick walls, red tile floors, beamed ceilings, and open fireplaces. Filled with Martha's Plains Indian baskets, rugs, and artifacts, it has just the informal atmosphere we wanted in our desert home.

We spend every weekend in Palm Springs and I am happiest there, never more relaxed or more comfortable. Martha and I walk on the golf course with our dog, watch football or other sporting events on TV, sit in the sun, golf, have massages, enjoy our hot tub and life in general.

Martha has been very good for me. We like the same things. We suit each other.

Rarely does a man find the one right woman to marry.

I was blessed.

I found two.

(Hal's first wife was Louise Fazenda, the much-loved silent film comedienne. She was admired and respected by all who knew her.)

Life with Hal was exciting. There was never a dull moment, or a free one. I was busy from sunup to sundown with lists, plans, and schedules. I was a loving wife, an involved community figure, chatelaine of three homes, a caring friend and relative, an indefatigable hostess.

We entertained the greats of the world—presidents and cabinet members, heads of state, famous authors, film directors, and stars. I had to dress properly for all occasions, and see that Hal did, too. As the years went by, he depended on me more and more to organize and coordinate our very active lives.

I realized how fortunate I was to have such a nearly perfect marriage, but I hated its dark underside. My secret struggle to support our life-style slowly destroyed my pleasure in it. I tried to forget my problems by filling the days with activity—meetings, fittings, interior decorating, ladies' luncheons. But in the dark of the night, I couldn't forget. Guilt-ridden and wracked with anxiety, I prayed, "Let it be all right. Help me not to hurt him. Please."

There are reels of film in my head of the happy side of life with Hal. I run them constantly.

I remember his kindness and loyalty to me. Whenever gorgeous, Hollywood-hungry girls threw themselves at him, he'd put his arm around me and give me his full attention, politely ignoring the auditioning ladies. He gave me dignity, as his girl and as his wife.

We loved traveling. Hawaii was our favorite spot—Mauna Kea in particular. On our way there from the airport in Hilo, we always stopped at a little country store to buy tropical fruit juices and snacks. At sundown, Hal would mix tall drinks of rum and passion-fruit juice for us to sip on our deck overlooking Mauna Kea's perfect crescent beach and turquoise sea. Paradise.

After one trip, we had cases of passion-fruit juice shipped to our home in Palm Springs so we could duplicate the tropical drinks there. One day, I noticed the cases were gone. When I questioned my young day helper, she confessed, "Oh, Mrs. Wallis, I drank every can. I needed it so badly. And it's helped me! I'm much more passionate now."

I loved being with Hal on location trips. He made Elvis's *Blue Hawaii* in Kauai, *Barefoot in the Park* with Jane Fonda and Robert Redford in New York, *True Grit* in Colorado, and *Red Sky at Morning* in Santa Fe, which began our lifelong love affair with this very special city. We delighted in its beauty, antiquity, and mysticism. The Indians say Santa Fe is sacred ground. I believe it.

I'll never forget Hal's loving solicitude when my mother and father died. They lived in Dallas, where my father was judge of the 44th District Court. Their lives were long and happy, but I was heartsick over losing them. I don't know what I would have done without my husband's love and strength and compassion.

Our married life was nearly perfect. During the twenty years we were married, Hal never looked at another woman, nor I at another man. We had everything we wanted in each other. He was the star, and I liked it that way. It was fascinating being behind the scenes at the very highest level of the picture business. His position garnered all respect, all services. When we traveled, representatives of studios met us to smooth out travel inconveniences. We saw new films before they were released in our private screening room at home, run by a projectionist from the studio.

A typical dinner party chez Wallis began with cocktails and hors d'oeuvres around the bar, then a Chinese dinner in the oak-paneled dining room, followed by the screening of a new film. We had marvelous Chinese cooks, and a favorite ploy of mine was to write personal messages to insert in the fortune cookies (such as for Genevieve Bujold: "Prepare speech this spring; Oscar for *Anne* sure thing"—unfortunately, Confucius was wrong that time).

Hal was the first producer to put Elvis Presley under contract, and the best pictures Elvis made were Hal Wallis productions. Elvis admired Hal very much—always respectfully addressed him as "Sir." He and his manager, Colonel Tom Parker, had dinner with us in our homes several times. Elvis liked only junk food and was too restless to sit at a table for long. He was soft-spoken, well mannered, and gentlemanly. His shyness and lack of small talk led him to avoid social situations he could not control.

With all the fame, all the adulation, Elvis was basically a very insecure person. He refused to go without a shirt in some of Hal's films because he was ashamed of his thin arms and underdeveloped chest.

Hal and Colonel Parker were fast friends. Hal trusted him. They had only a handshake deal for Elvis's services, and they both honored it.

One weekend, Elvis invited us to his opening in Las Vegas. We went backstage to congratulate him after the performance. During our conversation, Hal directed a few personal remarks to me. Elvis turned abruptly and left us. If a conversation did not concern him, he wanted no part of it.

But he was incredibly generous, always helping those

less fortunate. And there was a spiritual side to Elvis. He felt himself guided by an inner light. He studied and read constantly in his search for spiritual enlightenment.

I don't think he was a drug addict per se. I firmly believe Elvis "doctored" himself for what he thought were health reasons—and overdid it.

Hal Wallis was a very possessive man. He wanted his wife with him as much of the time as possible. He even resented the few days I spent each year with my family in Texas, and wasn't keen on their visiting me. For nearly twenty years, his family replaced mine on an almost-daily basis, including weekends and holidays. I loved my husband very much. I adjusted.

Minna Wallis, Hal's sister, was famous in her own right as a top Hollywood agent and a colorful character. She was a good friend of mine until she found out Hal might marry me. Then she became a problem. I never took her enmity personally. I realized she would have felt the same way about anyone Hal dated. She was extremely possessive and loved him inordinately.

Later in our married life, Minna and I became very fond of each other. We saw so much of her that Hal used to say, "Remember the good old days when Minna wasn't speaking to us?"

She was a loyal friend to Clark Gable, Greta Garbo, Ava Gardner, Anne and Kirk Douglas, Myrna Loy, Roddy McDowall, the Sinatras, and Merle Oberon, among others.

She was short in stature, eccentric, rotund, ate everything in sight (particularly sweets), never dieted, never exercised, washed her sleeping pills down with vodka, never had a checkup, was a Type-A worrier, and passed peacefully from this world at the age of ninety-four, never having suffered a sick day in her life. Good genes.

There is one Minna story that must be updated. In 1959, Hal decided to bid on a beautiful Impressionist pastel by Degas being auctioned at the Thelma Chrysler Foy sale in New York. He had planned a trip out of the country at the time of the auction so empowered Minna to bid on the picture for him. He told her to bid between $80,000 and $100,000.

The day of the sale, Hal was sunning on the beach in Nassau when he was paged for an overseas call from his partner, Joe Hazen. Joe told him that the Degas had gone for the highest price ever paid for a painting by that artist.

Hal: "How much?"

Joe: "One hundred eighty thousand dollars."

Hal: "Who bought it?"

Joe: "You did."

Hal broke out in a cold sweat. Instead of bidding between $80,000 and $100,000, Minna had reversed the numbers and combined them to bid $180,000. Hal was furious and never let her forget it.

Cut to May 10, 1989, Christie's Auction House, New York City. The Hal Wallis collection is being sold to benefit the Hal Wallis Foundation. That same Degas pastel drawing, entitled *Sur la Scène,* sells for $6.6 million.

Minna, wherever you are, I hope you know—*you did good!*

In passing, I have to mention that Hal Wallis was also a pack rat—he never wanted to throw anything away.

When we married in 1966, I found stacks of *National Geographics* in his bedroom dating back to the forties. Going through his closets, I asked him on what occasions he wore certain strange jackets and shirts. He replied, "When I play polo with Darryl Zanuck." Since those games took place in the 1930s, I felt free to call Goodwill.

The huge basement of our beautiful South Mapleton Drive home was another story. It was stacked to the ceiling with newspapers, boxes, mementos, broken lamps, old furniture, and assorted junk.

One day, I very quietly called UCLA and arranged to donate a large part of the rubbish to their annual rummage sale (two truckloads, to be exact). I didn't say anything about it to my husband. Weeks later, we attended the sale, and Hal unknowingly bought back practically every piece I'd donated! So much for a clean sweep.

True Grit, Hal's classic Western, was a huge success, special from the start. Maybe once in an actor's lifetime the perfect part for him comes along, if he's lucky. This was it for Duke. At the Academy Awards that year, Hal's two pictures, *Anne of the Thousand Days* and *True Grit,* shared more than a dozen nominations. We didn't know who to root for, but knew we couldn't lose. I think Duke's award was one of the most popular ever given.

I was proud to be with Hal as he was made a commander of the British empire. He was honored also with an honorary doctor's degree by Northwestern University and with retrospectives of his work at the Museum of Art in New York, the National Film Theatre in London, the French Cinematheque in Paris, the County Museum of Art in Los Angeles, and the Desert Museum in Palm Springs, California—all glowing tributes to a man who helped shape American film.

Hal had always been a very private person socially. After we were married, he discovered he liked people and enjoyed some parties and entertaining in his home.

He became a member of the board of trustees of the Los Angeles County Museum of Art, and, as his wife, I became a vice president of the Blue Ribbon Four Hundred of the Music Center, a trustee of Northwestern University, a board member of the Natural History Museum of Los Angeles and the Eisenhower Medical Center in Rancho Mirage, California.

When the Prince of Wales made a trip from Australia to California on a naval training cruise, Hal and I were invited to attend a party for him on board his ship in San Diego harbor.

We stayed at the stately old Coronado Hotel and were honored to meet and converse with the future king of England. He was warm, witty, and very bright. Full of questions about Hollywood, he lamented the fact that no visit there had been scheduled for him.

"I think that can be arranged, sir," promised Hal, who immediately set about producing such a visit.

The next day, Prince Charles and his attendants arrived at Universal Studios in a fleet of limousines. Hal hosted a beautiful luncheon with a star-studded guest list and a private tour of the studio.

Very quietly, the prince confided his longing to meet "my Hollywood dream girl—Barbra Streisand." Hal arranged that, too. The meeting was a great success. They were intrigued with each other, proving that opposites do attract. I said to her, "It looks like you're going to play the Palace." And she did. I believe shortly thereafter she sang at a royal charity benefit in London and was invited to tea at Buckingham Palace.

We spent wonderful years in England while Hal produced *Becket, Anne of the Thousand Days, Mary, Queen of Scots, The Nelson Affair,* and *The Public Eye.*

We loved every minute of our life in London. We lived in a suite at the Dorchester and dined often at the Mirabelle or the Connaught. Saturdays we lunched on our private terrace after gourmet shopping at Fortnum's. Hal was chauffeured to the studio every day while I shopped and savored London.

We had trips to the south of France to La Reserve in Beaulieu and visited the David Nivens at their villa on Cap Ferrat. We explored Normandy, adored Honfleur, and had memorable Mediterranean cruises on the Richard Dutton-Forshaws' yacht, *The Cardigrae.* We spent weekends in Majorca, Venice, Salzburg.

I teased Hal that he only took me to Paris on weekends or in August when the shops were closed. But I couldn't complain—we stayed at the Ritz and dined at restaurants like Taillevent and Grand Vefour.

When Peter Finch was starring for Hal in *The Nelson Affair,* I called his wife, Eleta, to invite them to dinner at the Guinea, an informal American-type restaurant that served great steaks. We agreed to meet at our suite at the Dorchester. They arrived dressed very elegantly, almost formally. I remarked that they were too gorgeous for the Guinea, and Eleta cried, "The Guinea! My deah—I thought you said the Guinesses'." Peter took off his tie and socks immediately.

One night we went to the theater to see Anna Magnani in *El Lupo.* She had starred for Hal in *The Rose Tattoo,* and they were fast friends.

The play was performed in Italian, so each seat was equipped with earphones through which an interpreter translated the dialogue being spoken onstage into English. It was hilarious. Hal and I could hardly keep straight faces.

The fiery Magnani would yell, scream, practically tear the place apart. Then, with a cultured British upper-class accent, the interpreter would translate it into something like, "I say, are you going on holiday? What shocking weather we're having"—words ludicrously different from the Italian intent.

We didn't mention this when we went backstage after the show. Anna saw Hal across the dressing room, screamed, "Hol," and charged. She threw herself on him, her legs locked around his waist. (His back was never the same.)

She was in her late sixties then but came to see us at the Dorchester in a black leather micromini skirt, a revealing tank top (no bra), and long black hair, with underarm growth to match.

Anna Magnani generated electricity like a lightning bolt. When she was around, *you knew it.*

We attended royal command performances of Hal's films, met Her Majesty the queen, Prince Philip, the Queen Mother, and Princess Anne. Lord Gavin Astor and his family became warm, special friends. We met them when they graciously allowed us to shoot scenes for *Anne of the Thousand Days* at their historic Hever Castle in Kent. They invited us to go grouse shooting on the moors of their home in Scotland, a never-to-be-forgotten weekend.

During the filming of *Anne,* Elizabeth Taylor and Richard Burton lived in the penthouse suite next to us at the Dorchester Hotel in London. I had known Elizabeth since she was a teenager. Marshall Thompson and I attended her sixteenth birthday party when her parents gifted her with her first car. Even then, people stopped cold when they saw her, stunned by her beauty. She was told repeatedly, "You are the most beautiful girl in the world."

So I was pleasantly surprised by the woman she'd become. With that legacy, it couldn't have been easy to have had any kind of normal life, but somehow she's managed to retain a soft sweetness at her core, no matter how hard the veneer. Behind the image of diamonds, yachts, glamour, and luxury lives a giving spirit dedicated to her family and to anyone who needs her help.

Hal and I marveled at how well and happy Maria Burton was. She is the daughter Richard and Elizabeth adopted who was born with a crippling hip deformity. Elizabeth wanted her especially because she knew she could help her. After many expensive operations, Maria recovered. Today she is a beautiful and healthy young lady.

On Hal's film *Becket,* director Peter Glenville told us that Elizabeth very quietly arranged for one of England's finest surgeons to operate on an assistant's crippled son, curing him completely.

Hal kept me up on all the intrigue during the filming of *Anne.* Richard and Genevieve Bujold engaged in a flirtation that infuriated Elizabeth. She haunted the set to keep an eye on them. Just before doing her biggest scene in the film, Genevieve was heard to say, "I'll give that bitch an acting lesson she'll never forget."

When the picture was finished, so was the flirtation. That was Richard's MO.

The single most beautiful party I have ever enjoyed was one given by the American ambassador to the Court of St. James, Walter Annenberg, and his wife, Lee. It was held at the embassy residence to mark the end of their very successful tenure in London. The weather was perfect, warm and balmy. There were tables inside and out on the terrace, a full moon, a gazebo, flowers everywhere, orchestras flown in from America and the Continent, fantastic food, the finest wines. The guest list included not only members of the royal family but first families from America and abroad as well. The evening was perfect.

While filming *The Public Eye* in England, Hal and I came to know and love Mia Farrow. He had wanted her for the lead in *True Grit.* She'd accepted, then declined after hearing stories about how difficult it was to work with director Henry Hathaway. She preferred Roman Polanski, who'd just directed her in *Rosemary's Baby,* but Hal wouldn't budge (fortunately). She admitted later that it was the biggest mistake of her career.

During the filming of *The Public Eye,* Mia invited us to a picnic at her home in Surrey. We motored down from London to her enchanted cottage—everybody's dream of what an English farmhouse should be.

Mia was married to André Prévin, and their children were adorable. They helped us pack the picnic lunch and quilts into a wheelbarrow. Mia wheeled away like the Pied Piper as we followed her to a dell in the woods overlooking a meadow of field flowers. Even rough-it-at-the-Waldorf Hal Wallis loved that picnic.

I'm convinced the fairies kissed Mia awake. She is fey, fun, and marches to a very special different drummer.

Another memorable experience Hal and I shared was the making of the film *Rooster Cogburn* in Oregon with John Wayne and Katharine Hepburn. Just thinking about it makes me happy because it brings back memories of Kate. She is a knockout, probably the greatest lady I've ever known, maybe that the world has ever known. Becoming her friend was reality exceeding my dreams. After being a worshipful fan for years, I was nervous that it might be hard to relate to her on the same social level. No problem. She became a warm, personal friend and has remained so until this day. As a matter of fact, she and Hal were such a mutual admiration society that if it had been twenty years earlier, look out, Martha!

Rooster Cogburn was a sequel to *True Grit.* John Wayne played the one-eyed marshal, and Kate played a strong, sensitive pioneer woman.

Hal had great difficulty getting a shootable script. He knew what he wanted, so he and I wrote the first draft of the screenplay. Then Duke and Kate rewrote parts of it, and later Charles Portis—author of *True Grit* and originator of the Cogburn character—put a polish on it.

Hal and I had script conferences with Duke at his Newport Beach house. One day, there were several young fans on tricycles outside his front door. When he appeared, toupéeless, one cried, "Mr. Wayne, Mr. Wayne, what happened to your hair?" Without missing a beat, Duke replied, "Oh, the Indians got it, Sonny. They scalped me."

The picture was filmed in Oregon—the rapids sequence was shot on the Rogue River near Grant's Pass. Hal and I traveled there by way of mystically beautiful Crater Lake.

From our motel room in Grant's Pass, Hal called Kate to say hello. She told him she'd arrived the night before, had spent the day checking out the locations, swimming in the Rogue River, riding the rapids in a raft, and buying a kayak she planned to use between shots.

She and Phyllis, her secretary-companion, thanked him for the flowers, cheese, and Scotch whiskey he'd sent to welcome them. Hal said, "Well, I thought you might like a little nip occasionally." Kate laughed. "Occasionally! We finished half the bottle the first night."

We went up to her rooms overlooking the river, a simple suite equipped with a refrigerator and hot plate so that she could have her meals there. There were books around, personal mementos, pictures—the stamp of her personality was already on everything. It was a home. On the table was a bowl of freshly picked blueberries and a dish of homegrown radishes, gifts of the motel manager.

Kate is such a private person, she does not like to eat in restaurants. I don't blame her—she'd be mobbed. Even in Oregon, people came up on the street to touch her and say, "I love you." She was always gracious and laughed it off later with, "I should be in the Aimee Semple McPherson business."

On the first day of shooting, Kate had her little hideaway dressing room, constructed of canvas flats, set up upriver. She preferred this to a trailer. She stayed there until called, swimming, eating, and rowing in her kayak.

She was like a billy goat tramping up and down the steep hills. When the wardrobe woman cautioned her, she said, "Leave me alone, Agnes. I am aging my shoes."

She was independent, enthusiastic, sharp, witty, unique. At the end of the day, when Duke complained that he was dragging, she felt great. Ageless. When Duke couldn't remember his lines, she cued him. When he overacted, she warned him, "You're tippin' your mitt, old boy. Save the mugging for when it means something." After running the rapids in her kayak "to prove to myself that I could do it," she regretted that she'd bought the twenty-one-foot boat. "They had a forty-one-foot one that I should have bought. This one is a little small." She said she wanted to see and do everything—experience it all—because she felt time was running out on her. It wouldn't dare.

One day over a picnic lunch, Kate told us how fascinated she was by Duke. "I love working with him," she said with a twinkle in her eye, "but he bullies everyone, takes charge of the set, and I'm the one who usually does that." Hal came right back with, "Next time he thinks he knows everything, remind him of *The Alamo* and *The Green Berets.*"

Duke was miserable at that altitude and often made everyone else miserable. He couldn't take a drink at night because he was on medication, and that made him cross. He couldn't sleep, coughed constantly, needed oxygen, and was emotionally upset because of his breakup with his wife, Pilar. He took out his unhappiness on everyone.

Kate called herself "Miss Kissinger" and got along fine with Duke no matter what the situation. One evening, she compared him with Spencer Tracy—both excellent actors, both professional, but she felt Spence the more intuitive, the more disciplined. She said Tracy never changed a word once he accepted a script. But he could be deadly, even tougher than Duke. He could zero in ruthlessly, but never on someone who was weak.

She said Hal reminded her of Spence, too. When she saw a picture of Hal taken in 1959, she said, "Is this you? You looked so silly then, and so marvelous now, handsome and distinguished. I told Spence the same. He looked even better as he got older." It was a mutual admiration society of the highest order. I have a photo of Kate and Hal looking at each other with such affection that Kate autographed it, "If looks could talk—what volumes!"

A *Time* magazine writer visited the set one day. Duke was the perfect gentleman for a while, but couldn't sustain it. "I'm glad you're leaving," he told him. "Now I don't have to be nice anymore." Things quickly reverted to normal.

But when he played the cigar-smoking scene around the campfire, Duke purred. He relished it—said he hadn't had a cigar since *Katie Elder* and never enjoyed anything more. It was his best scene in the picture.

After one particularly trying day—Duke screaming at people, blowing up over nothing—he came to Hal's room all cowboyish charm. "I hear you're mad at me," he said, grinning sheepishly. All was forgiven.

Life magazine sent a photographer to do a layout of Kate on location. The pictures were fabulous. She looked about twenty-one. It was obvious the cameraman—and the camera—was in love with her. She had a clause in her contract that allowed her to approve her publicity. It was not that she objected to publicity, but she wanted the right kind. She wanted to look well in the pictures, do them right, and not have them interfere with her work. She is a smart lady, a perfectionist in the best sense of the word.

Duke ad-libbed a lot—too much. When the director called him on it, he was furious. "What are you trying to do—take away my character?" He said he hadn't said the exact words of any script since he worked for Mascot Productions early in his career. He improvised his dialogue, using modern expressions and words that destroyed completely the flavor and rhythm of the quaint speeches written by Charles Portis.

Kate was just the opposite. When the director asked her to improvise one day—to say whatever she felt—she said she was sorry but she didn't work that way. When he wanted her to play a scene a certain way, she said, "It doesn't matter. I'll play me. Duke will play him. We'll do what we always do. It'll be fine."

Sitting on the set one day, with my eyes closed, I realized most of the moviegoing public would know Duke's and Kate's voices in the dark. Their sounds are unique—and so are their souls.

A member of the crew confided to me that Hepburn reads to the blind regularly, and very privately visits people who are ill, imbuing them with her strength and spirit. When Susan Hayward was dying, Kate visited her in her home daily. She has an open account in a shop in Westwood Village to provide canes to all who cannot afford them.

The crew member also told me that under the gruff, macho front of John Wayne was hidden a heart of gold. He said if you were Wayne's friend, you learned the true meaning of the word. Duke gave a permanent job as his production assistant to Paul Fix, who had been his drama coach in 1929. When George Coleman, in charge of his company's transportation, was injured by a drunk in a Mexican bar, Duke set him up in a car-rental business. And after Harry

Carey, Sr., died, his widow, "Ollie," always had an acting job with Wayne.

When the river scenes were finished in Grant's Pass, we moved to Sunriver Ranch Resort in Bend, Oregon. Kate and Phyllis had a meadow house next to ours with breathtaking views of the Three Sisters Mountains.

The first morning there, Hal said, "Guess who's coming to dinner?" Before I left for location, I made a stew, pulled lettuce for a salad, and set the table with an antique cotton quilt and candles stuck in pieces of gnarled wood. Kate and Phyllis brought wildflowers from the mountains. I put a loaf of French bread, wine, and cheese on the table, there was a beautiful sunset, and we had a wonderful time. The four of us had many memorable evenings in their cottage and in ours. Sometimes Phyllis cooked, other nights I did. There was always a roaring fire, good food, good wine, good conversation.

One night we talked about Howard Hughes. Kate went with him for years—he used to visit her in Connecticut. He was an expert golfer, and so was she. She packed sandwiches for him when he flew around the world. She felt he was eccentric because he couldn't hear from the time he was fifteen but wouldn't admit it. Hal told his Hughes story—how Howard insisted Hal leave Paramount to run RKO but would only meet him for conferences at Hal's sister's house after he'd checked out the closets, bedrooms, and baths for bugs (both kinds, I'm sure).

Kate told us stories about playing in *Coco* in New York and on the road. Director Tony Harvey came to visit, and he told marvelous tales of making *The Lion in Winter* with Kate.

One night, we discussed the new technique of babies being born underwater to ease the trauma of birth. Kate said that was absolute rot. They should be slapped immediately so they won't be surprised when the world starts doing it.

Kate's best story was about *The Philadelphia Story.* She had been labeled box-office poison by Hollywood, so she went to Broadway and was a smash hit in *The Philadelphia Story.* She bought the film rights before agreeing to appear in it. L. B. Mayer liked the property and said he would buy it for Norma Shearer. Kate said no—she wanted to do it herself with Gable and Tracy. (She hadn't yet met Tracy.) Mayer said fine if the two actors agreed. They didn't. He said he would let her write, produce, direct—anything but act in it. Kate was adamant. Finally Mayer said the only actor he could *make* do it was Jimmy Stewart. Kate said fine, then called Cary Grant and asked him to do the other male role for old times' sake. He said he would if it could be done in a four-week period between commitments he had, and he wanted top billing (he was always billed below her in their films at RKO). She said okay, and screen history was made. The movie was a tremendous success, a classic. She was nominated for an Oscar, her career reactivated.

When Kate read *Gone with the Wind* in galleys, she asked RKO to buy it for her (for $50,000). Executives there said the role of Scarlett was not sympathetic enough—it was not a leading woman's role.

One day she went by David Selznick's house. He was reading the book, and she said, "Don't read it—buy it." After he did and started the Scarlett search, he said he wanted to test her for it. She said, "David, if I test for it, I'll get it. You'll sign me, and then five days before the picture starts, you'll find the young unknown you've been looking for and pay me off and ruin my career. If you don't find anyone five days before you start, come back to me and I'll do it. Walter Plunkett can make costumes for me overnight. George [Cukor, the original director of *Gone with the Wind*] knows I am a quick study." Selznick found Vivien Leigh exactly five days before the film was to begin shooting.

At Sunriver, Duke lived in the owner's hideaway, complete with swimming pool and a private putting green. On Hal's birthday, he invited us all to a party there and was a warm, gracious host.

Duke's friend Canlis, a famous restaurateur from Seattle, flew in to do the cooking, and it was fabulous: poached salmon, exotic salads, garlic shrimp to suck and shuck, multiple birthday cakes, the finest champagne.

My birthday toast to Hal was, "To the youngest man I know."

Kate added, "To a man who has a lot of nerve."

"Chutzpah," I corrected her with a smile.

Kate was nose-up about going to the party, and only went because it was Hal's birthday. But once there, she had more fun than anybody and made the evening special for all of us. She wore her Rebel hat, hair tucked under it, pants, scarf, and shirt—her uniform. Duke kidded her about her strong drinks. She told him she drank Tracy and George Stevens under the table. She also told him, "I'm glad I didn't know you with two lungs. You really must have been a bastard. You're a monster with just one." Duke said he couldn't fight back because he'd promised John Ford to be nice to her. He was in great form—told stories about John Huston on the set of *The Barbarian and the Geisha* and was his old self. We sang "Happy Birthday" to Hal under the stars. He never forgot it.

When I was in bed with the flu, Kate brought me chicken soup, French bread, and sweet butter. I asked her to thank

Phyllis for me. She said, "I will not. Don't give her all the credit. I cut up those vegetables myself and contributed a lot to that soup."

One day Hal got a frantic call from Duke. His children were visiting him, and one of them hit him in the eye with a gold club as he was teaching her how to swing. His eye was bruised, discolored, and badly cut. "It's just your luck, you son of a bitch!" he yelled. "The eye she hit is the one with the patch on it." (The role Duke played was a one-eyed marshal who wore a black eye patch.)

The weather in Oregon was incredibly beautiful. One hundred perfect days. Wallis weather.

Kate went swimming in the waterfalls, visited the salmon hatcheries, and came to the locations even when she wasn't involved in the scenes.

After dinner one night, Kate told a group of us a story about Hal. He'd called to discuss her doing *Summer and Smoke* for him. When she told him how much salary she wanted, she never heard from him again. When she told this to George Cukor, he said, "That's nothing. Once I was talking a deal with him, and when I told him how much I wanted, he hung up while I was still talking." We all laughed. Hal denied it. I believed it. I'd been there! I could top those stories of his penuriousness with a few of my own.

For the end-of-the-picture party, I borrowed a beautiful house with a huge fireplace and a lovely kitchen, and invited the entire cast and crew as Hal's guests. We made arrows with stars on them to point the way and put a Duke-o'-lantern on a lamppost by the door. The pumpkin had a patch over one eye, Duke's red bandanna around its neck, and his cowboy hat on top. Crew members cooked their specialties, and I made guacamole and the tollhouse cookies Kate and Duke adored. Duke called them corn dodgers after the saddlebag biscuits his character shot up in the picture. Neighbors got into the spirit by sending tasty contributions to the party. I remember that a poppy-seed cake from an old German recipe was a standout.

Duke loved it all but couldn't breathe. He was scared—gasping, wheezing, miserable. We sent to Bend for oxygen tanks, and he went home to bed.

Kate was in rare form. She entertained us with stories of her early days at RKO. She said she always read everybody's mail and one day happened to pick up the script of *Morning Glory* off Pan Berman's desk. She took it home, read it, and called him to say, "I am going to do this. It is just right for me." He said it was meant for Constance Bennett. Kate said, "It is wrong for her—perfect for me." It was. She used the voice pattern of her friend Ruth Gordon for the character she played in *Morning Glory*—one level, a monotone. Everybody loved it and started imitating her. She sent Ruth Gordon a telegram saying, "Thank you very much."

Hal and I planned to leave location on a chartered Continental 727 jet from Medford the day before the crew left. Kate told Hal, "I know your plans. I have my spies. You are going to go to Portland and fly from there commercial while we take the charter and will all be killed." She told him, "Be sure there is enough liquor on board so that we will all have a good time and the crew will be happy."

Kate and Phyllis had us over for a farewell dinner: fresh stream-caught salmon, gazpacho, beef Stroganoff, rice, salad and cheese, baked pears—all superb. Kate looked divine in a bright red robe and a white turtleneck. She presented us with a gift I treasure—a handmade pewter pillbox with the sun on top and on the bottom the inscription, "To Hal and Martha from Kate—Love—1974."

Kate shared wonderful times with us at our beach house in Malibu. Hal and I had been spending our winters in Palm Springs and our summers in rented beach houses. When property we liked became available in Trancas, we built our own place and enjoyed it for many years. Close friends like Dona and Lou Lichtenfield, Joy and Edd Henry, Selma and Carl Pearl, Kate and Charles Jarrott, Helen and Dick Wolford, Radie Harris, Hepburn, and Phyllis all helped make Hal's golden years even more golden.

I remember that one summer at the beach Hal requested a high-class junk-food birthday dinner of guacamole, Dom Perignon champagne, Chasen's chili, and Baskin-Robbins ice cream. He got it—with a gift-wrapped roll of Di-Gel.

For another birthday, I made a video for Hal. As background music, I paraphrased the lyrics of "Mame" and had a singing group record them. Then Chuck Stabile helped me put together a collection of still photographs that flashed the story of Hal's life on-screen as the audio played back "Haaal." He loved it.

(With apologies to Jerry Herman)

Hal

You made us all so proud to know you—Haaal
We'll all be friends forever with you—Haaal
You've got the style, the magic

Your films will live as long as classics should
The whole world's been applauding
Since you first put the H in Hollywood.

You found the stars and gave them their
fame—Haaal
You won the prize and Oscar's his name—Haaal
You cast, you filmed, you made it
You decided what was in and what was not
And when we asked for more from you
True Grit and other greats was what we got

You made the competition look sad—Haaal
You showed 'em all what talent you had—Haaal
You came, you saw, you conquered and
Absolutely nothing is the same
Your special fascination'll prove inspirational
We think you're just sensational
Hal!
Happy Birthday

There are only a few evenings of our good life that I'd like to forget. One took place in 1971 when President Nixon was in Palm Springs for the dedication of the Eisenhower Medical Center. He was accompanied by his secretary of state, Henry Kissinger, the most fascinating and talked-about man in government at the time.

A high-ranking Republican asked Hal if we would have a dinner party for Kissinger—he would like to meet the film people there for the festivities.

I invited the Gregory Pecks, the Sinatras, Lucille Ball and Gary Morton, Greer Garson and Buddy Fogelson—every star in the area. I hired extra help, worked for days on the decorations and seating arrangement, and thought I had it all under control.

Half an hour before the guests were due to arrive, Kissinger called from San Clemente. The president wanted to return to Washington earlier than planned, so he would be unable to attend the party. I choked out how sorry I was, next time, and so forth. Then, sick at heart, I greeted my guests with the bad news. They were disappointed—they were there specifically to meet Kissinger—but they rallied and made the best of it. When they'd gone, I drank all the wine left in the glasses and vowed to vote the Democratic ticket next time.

Another night I wish I could forget took place at our home on Mapleton Drive in Los Angeles. Hal and I had just returned from London and planned an evening to screen *The Nelson Affair* for the MCA executives. The movie had been filmed and cut in England, and they had not yet seen it.

Nobody told Baby Martha that there were factions at the studio—gentlemen who did business with each other but did not mix socially. Knowing nothing of the politics involved, I invited the Jules Steins, the Lew Wassermans, the Taft Schreibers, and the Edd Henrys for dinner and the screening.

The first catastrophe: Hal developed a toothache, had the tooth removed the afternoon of the party, took to his bed, and told me he wouldn't be downstairs for the evening. I'd have to handle it.

The second catastrophe: The guests arrived, and the atmosphere grew frigid the minute they saw each other. I realized my faux pas and tried desperately to jolly everything along. No way. Only Doris Stein drank enough to relax a little.

Dinner, though delicious, was a disaster. Jules Stein couldn't eat chicken with morilles in champagne sauce and asked for scrambled eggs. Conversation was minimal. Naturally, they hated the film. No response, no laughs, no tears, no reaction—just cool thank-yous and good-nights as they rushed for the door. That night, I didn't just drink up the wine left in the glasses—I cleaned out the cellar!

In Rancho Mirage, we had many wonderful evenings at home with our friends. Chinese dinners were enjoyed by the Reagans, the Gerald Fords, the Annenbergs, the Sinatras, the Firestones, and yes—eventually—the Kissingers.

When Nancy and Henry Kissinger were houseguests, our Chinese cook, Cheung, and his housekeeper wife, Atsun, took very good care of them.

There was a Jacuzzi in the bathroom, and one day Henry asked Atsun to draw his bath. She underestimated the potency of the bubble bath, and the small room filled with foam—wall-to-wall bubbles. Henry stepped into the tub, then teased her that he expected her to scrub his back. She averted her eyes, put her hand over her mouth, and fled crying, "Me Chinese—not Japanese."

Cheung and Atsun adored him and his sense of humor. When they packed his bags, he told them to pack another one for them—he was taking them back to Washington with him.

But our phones were never the same again. A hot-line switchboard that was as complicated as the control panel of a jet had been set up in the command-post guest house. The Secret Service had patrolled the grounds and reported that one evening, Frank Sinatra, who lived directly across from us, strolled across the fairway for a visit at the exact moment the automatic sprinklers on the golf course went on, resulting in a very soaked Sinatra.

8

AFTER THE FALL—AN AWAKENING

This then was the exciting life I was trying to hold on to at any cost. As late as 1980, it still appeared perfect on the surface. But the ugly undercurrent of my deception slowly sucked the happiness out of it.

Stress and anxiety became my constant companions, taking all the joy out of what should have been vintage years. My problems never got better, only worse. Helplessly, I fell in a long spiral downward into the depths of despair until that traumatic night at Trancas, the turning point of my life.

The morning after it happened was like any other beach morning. Hal and I had breakfast between tubs of daisies and red geraniums on our tree-shaded brick terrace. After he finished his coffee and his paper, I asked him to take a walk with me along the shore. He realized the seriousness of the request when I refused to let Missy, my beloved Yorkie, join us.

As we sat on the dunes, holding hands, looking out over a placid, breakerless sea, I found the courage to tell him how I had abused his trust, wasted his resources, taken advantage of his love. I unburdened my soul.

Hal was known for never showing emotion, and I saw no reaction on his stern profile as I spoke slowly into his good right ear. But his blue eyes brimmed with tears as he turned to me and asked, "Is there someone else?"

"No, darling, and there never will be," I cried as we hugged and sobbed and held each other so close we were one heartbeat, one body, bonded.

There were no recriminations on his part—no "how could you," only "how can we fix it?" He forgave me. I had always believed that if Hal knew the extent of my deception, I would lose him forever. Instead, he shouldered part of the blame, realized his mistakes, understood mine. He stood by me.

He hired fine lawyers at great expense to try to right my wrongs. Their investigators uncovered a web of duplicity and double-dealing that could have cost us our homes, a fortune, my very freedom. I was not the only victim of these swindlers. We asked the FBI for help, and as a result, many of the criminals involved are behind bars today. Others settled with us when threatened with exposure. The cost ran into millions.

This ordeal brought Hal and I even closer together. Our relationship was strengthened by the anguish we shared. We both changed, as did our priorities. We realized that our worship of money—our different concepts of its value—had come very close to destroying our lives.

Hal began to share his wealth, funding a research center at the Eisenhower Medical Center in Rancho Mirage, California, and a theater at Northwestern University in Evanston, Illinois. He increased my allowance and raised the salaries of all his employees. He opened his heart as he discovered that giving is the highest form of love and love is what life is all about.

Free from fear at last, I felt an overwhelming need to simplify my life. Things that had seemed important—position, image, material riches—lost all appeal. I devoted myself to my husband; not many men would have rescued me as he had.

Support, love, shared courage in the face of calamity—that's what marriage should be in the best sense of the word. That's what ours was. Hal never let me down. And in the years to come, I never let him down. Never again.

During those troubled times, I found solace in the memory of my God-experience, a cherished secret. I longed to confide in Hal but thought better of it under the circumstances. He was intent on unraveling our tangled financial affairs, and I knew he had little use for the spiritual, none for the supernatural.

One late night in the darkness of my Holmby Hills bedroom, I thought about how my values had changed, how my whole life was changing.

The room I was in had been designed by Michael Taylor, papered with Chinese panels handpainted in the eighteenth century. Scalamandre floral-patterned silk covered the sofa. The black-lacquered, ormolued desk and commode were priceless. A large picture window overlooked acres of trees, gardens, and an Olympic-sized swimming pool. I had been so proud of it all once. Now nothing mattered to me but the miracle I had experienced at Trancas.

I relived again the wonder of that night, marveled that I had been shown proof of my belief in a power greater than the human dimension. Was my life-shattering crisis His will—to bring me finally to Him? For if my life had remained perfect and wonderful, my hand would never have reached out so desperately to Him for help. Without experiencing the depths, can we ever attain the heights? I felt a deep-seated need for answers.

Then, once again, my hands began to tingle. There was a gentle brush against my neck, like a kiss. Warm white light infused my being. A profound sense of love washed over me. Slowly, but firmly, a force of energy lifted my body up from the bed. I was suspended above it briefly, then lowered gently back down.

Shaken, my heart hammering, I searched for meaning in the experience. Was it to show me the power of Spirit? His dominion over all? Where would I find an explanation? Who would understand? Troubled and more than a little frightened, I slept not at all that night.

The next day was a normal one, but there was a difference in me. As I went about the house preparing for a party (cutting and arranging flowers, discussing the menu with our cook, telephoning Hal's studio for the name of the film to be shown after dinner), I felt a quickening in my body from time to time. It was a visceral contraction followed by a long, deep breath, like a sigh or a sense of release. I was to later learn that it is a conscious reminder of my oneness with the Source—the presence of God within me. I didn't know that then. And I was scared.

I put on a happy face for our guests that evening, ever the charming hostess. But after I bid them good night, and after my husband was asleep, I crept downstairs in my robe; in the solarium, in the moonlight, I prayed for Enlightenment.

From out of nowhere, I remembered a spiritually beautiful friend in Palm Springs whose life had been transformed by similar experiences. I recalled that when she had told me about them, she had given me a book. Where was it?

I hurried through our elegantly formal living room into the library. Its walls were lined with books, but as if divinely led, I walked straight to the shelf where three years earlier I had left *Living the Infinite Way* by Joel Goldsmith. That slim volume was to prove more valuable to me than all the material treasures I had sold my soul to acquire.

There was a card in the book: "You will know when you are ready for this. There are no accidents on the Path. Nothing takes place by chance. Everything is according to divine order."

I lit a fire, curled up in a leather armchair, and read through the night. When the pink light of dawn filtered through the shutters onto the pages of my book, I knew it wasn't just the beginning of a new day for me—it was the beginning of a new life.

I became a pilgrim on the Infinite Way. Joel Goldsmith's book explained exactly what had happened to me, how it can happen to everybody, and that this transition is the purpose of our lives. His teachings have no special religious connotation. They are based on revelations to be found in Oriental, Hebrew, and Christian scriptures alike.

The Infinite Way is a way of life, the contemplative way. It is based on the truth that the Kingdom of God is within us all, waiting to be recognized, of no purpose or benefit until we become consciously aware of Its presence through the God-experience, the surrender of control to the Spirit.

Hal and I left for Palm Springs that morning, and in the afternoon, while he was playing golf, I drove to the Smoke Tree Book Store to buy all thirty of Joel Goldsmith's works. I soaked them up like a sponge, underlining first with a yellow marking pen, then with a red one, then blue.

I learned that Goldsmith had died in 1964, leaving a legacy of inspirational books and teachings that have become more important every year as our society searches desperately for spiritual roots and values.

After experiencing an overwhelming impartation in 1928, Joel found himself in a new dimension—ordained to pass on the truth revealed to him. The purpose of his books is to share his joy, not convert. He is quick to point out that there are many paths leading to the same place. His is but one of them.

It was revealed to him that God lives as us—we are His instruments. He is our essence, not someone out there separate and apart from us. We are one, all part of the same Spirit. And we make contact with that Spirit, our inner source, when we turn within.

How to do that? Joel says meditation is the answer. It creates an inner calm, a centeredness, a vacuum in which the presence of God can announce Itself. He calls meditation the connecting link between our outer life and our inner self, which is God.

At first, I was put off by the word *meditation*. It brought to mind the flower children of the sixties—hippies and communes. But I learned that true meditation is not the same as transcendental meditation, which is only a form of self-hypnosis and cannot lead to God-experience.

What a great gift I had been given: realization of the presence of God within me through Grace. I did not have to study or meditate or make a conscious effort to feel this awareness. After my God-experience, it was just there—an actual force within me that makes Itself known in the ways I have described. (And you may be sure It reminds me if I don't refer back to It often enough.)

I am inwardly companioned now. I'll never be lonely again.

My life changed completely as Spirit took over. I lost all feelings of resentment and rage against those who had wronged me. No matter what the appearance, I began to behold the Spirit as a potential in every individual I met.

There was a falling away of pride and ambition. The ego loses power after contact with the Lifestream. I developed an even-greater appreciation of beauty, but with no sense of desire for possessions.

Minor physical problems I suffered cleared up without my really noticing how or when. But Hal noticed.

One day, with a penetrating look and raised eyebrows, he queried, "You're different. Are you born again?"

"No," I replied. "Reclaimed. Recycled."

I tried to discuss my new way of life with Hal. He listened awhile, then tuned out and in to a TV football game.

Religion is of the heart. It is probably impossible to give a religious instinct to anyone. It's something that takes place within a person when he or she is ready for the spiritual experience. Truth is presented to us when we are prepared to accept it.

There is an old saying that "when the pupil is ready, the teacher appears." That was certainly so in my case. To find the way to the spiritual life, a map of some kind is necessary. Joel Goldsmith's books provided that for me. The truths I found revealed in them changed and enriched my life.

He recommended that students start with *Living the Infinite Way*, then progress to *Practicing the Presence* and *The Art of Meditation*.

Seeking to understand why I had been blessed with the God-experience, I found the following truths from Joel's book *Living Between Two Worlds* significant:

> No one attains the spiritual heights except those who have been in the lowest depths. The reason for this desolation is that a greater, deeper light is coming. There must be an emptying out process before this greater light can come. The soul is touched by the divine light in two ways—through preparation in the individual's consciousness through centuries of development and through the touch of one already illumined.

I was still making mistakes in 1982 and 1983, trying my best to overcome many very human problems. But I found myself doing for and helping friends as I never had before.

A widowed friend who made exquisite clothes for the country club ladies in Palm Springs had a stroke on a trip to Switzerland. She had no living relatives. The police found my name and number in her book and asked me if I would accept responsibility for her. I did.

I spoke with the hospital in Zurich, wired funds for her bill, contacted the State Department to arrange her air transportation from Europe to the Desert Hospital. And when she arrived on a stretcher accompanied by a medical nurse, I met them and saw her admitted and settled in the stroke ward.

My daily visits to this woman prompted Hal to ask in exasperation, "Why are you doing this?" I shrugged and smiled. It would have been hard for him to understand that I was only an instrument—a transparency through which the Grace of God was operating. But I began to understand Albert Schweitzer's words, "The only ones really happy are those who have sought and found how to serve."

Because I believe now that the one Self that God is, you are and I am, I have lost my fear of death. Can the offspring of God be less immortal than God?

When my closest friend, Dona, was dying of cancer in 1984, I sat by her bed and tried to help her understand this. Frail and wasted, she said tearfully, "I still feel like a kid inside."

I agreed. "You are, dear. We are Spirit, not form—and Spirit never ages, never dies. Our bodies are just the vehicles our spirits travel around in, mobile homes used by the I of us. When a light globe burns out, don't we automatically replace it with another globe to harness the electricity that is still there? When the body wears out, Spirit discards it and simply changes form. The energy, the essence, life itself is never lost."

We're all afraid of the unknown, but it was revealed to Joel Goldsmith that death is just a transition into a different state of experience, like a larva becomes transformed into a butterfly. I believe now that the life I am living is God's, and I am perfectly willing for Him to take it anywhere at any time.

This belief enabled me to face a near-miss automobile crash on a Los Angeles freeway and an aborted takeoff of a

727 jet with equanimity. I am no longer afraid to die. I know my spirit is life eternal.

All of us ask the question, "Why, Lord? Why wars, accidents, poverty, pestilence, unanswered prayers?" Strife in the Middle East and Ireland seems never to end. Innocent children are shot by drive-by snipers, others starve in Ethiopia. Child abuse is rampant. Why?

The answer given to Joel is that God is not in the material world. He only functions when He is admitted to consciousness. If we do not make contact with God, God is still fulfilling Itself—but not in our experience. Man was created to show forth God's handiwork, His glory. But mankind is set on fulfilling its own desires, its own way. That is why there is no God's Grace in the human experience. We are Prodigals. When we surrender ourselves and submit to His will, we return to the Father's house. And when we do, life becomes beautiful.

I can attest to that. At the age of sixty-five, I am happier than I have ever been in my life. God is my abiding place now. Like E. T. and the Prodigal, I've come home.

I have lots of company. Millions of people all over the world are on a Spirit quest, searching for truth, meaning, and significance in their lives. An awakening is taking place. Never before have so many identified with the indwelling Spirit—the God power within us.

This quote from Greta Garbo to Raymond Daun in *Life* magazine in 1989 reveals this universal hunger:

> I wish to God I was religious, I wish I were assured, then I wouldn't be in such a mess and 50 billion other people wouldn't either. If I only knew what to focus on. You don't have to go to church, if you have

> it in you, you don't need nuttin'. . . . All you have to do is have it inside your small little chest. I envy people who do . . . they have something, they seem so unafraid, they have something.

You can have it, too. You don't have to be "good" to receive God's grace—it's just the opposite. Getting God's grace makes you good because when you make the contact, your sins are not only forgiven, they are healed. No matter what you've done or been, His grace is dependent only on the depth of your desire to make contact with Him at the center of your being.

Barbara Mary Muhl, a former pupil of Joel's and a brilliant, divinely inspired teacher in her own right, sums up the message of the Infinite Way in these words from her book *The Royal Road to Reality* (Christus Publishing, Newhall, California, 1982):

> Our goal through meditation and study is to live the spiritual way to the point where we actually make our own God contact. Having made that, we then have a God-governed life and our worries as human beings are over as of that time. . . . No one in the world ever knows or can know whether there is a God until he has experienced It. We can be hoping there is, or believing there is, or having faith there is, but none of us will ever know for sure until he has made individual contact with this indwelling Spirit which announces Itself to him, within him, and brings with that announcement the proof of Its own validity. . . . The real presence of God can announce Itself to you in a hundred different ways. . . . Once it has, signs follow. While you can't prove His presence by phenomena,

> you can prove that He has been there by the fruitage that will immediately follow in your life. You will be changed. You will be altered. Spirit will never leave you where it found you . . . you will be different. You will have turned and gone in a different direction.

Service was the direction my life took in 1985 and 1986. Spirit became my strength during the heartbreaking years of my husband's illness.

We spent most of those years in hospitals. I lived in the same room with him, sharing the agony and the indignities he suffered from diabetes. He was so courageous—as much a hero as any in his films. At home in Rancho Mirage, we had nurses around the clock and wonderful doctors from the Eisenhower Medical Center in attendance.

But on the morning of October 5, 1986, at the age of 88, Hal passed away peacefully in his sleep—an answered prayer.

One of the greatest tragedies in life is not knowing what you have until you lose it. What sometimes passes for grief is often nothing more than regret. That wasn't true in our case. Hal and I had always known what we had. And valued it. There were no regrets. We'd had it all—ups, downs, romance, excitement, life in the fast lane, life in the slow lane, laughter, tears, tragedy.

Ours was a love story in the old-fashioned sense of the word. We were a team. Devoted. I had lost my best friend, companion, and partner.

The media coverage of Hal's death was staggering. In newspaper tributes and television accolades, he was praised, lauded, honored as few men are. He would have loved it. The best reviews of his career.

The *New York Times* described him as a "walking major studio . . . widely regarded as a gentleman in a difficult business . . . straightforward, levelheaded, circumspect in his private life . . . recognized as one of the ablest producers in the motion picture business."

A *Los Angeles Times* headline read, "Wallis: Creative Force in the Film Industry for 6 Decades Dies," and Charles Champlin wrote, "Wallis was one of that thin, diminished band of formative pioneers who helped to shape the studio production system in the early 20's and beyond. His vision supplied the furnishings for several generations worth of memory and dream."

President Reagan wrote, "He was a gifted and dedicated artist who gave the world some of our greatest films. His talent, professionalism, and instinct for excellence were an inspiration to all of us who had the privilege of working with him."

Another obituary was headed simply, "Hal Wallis: Gentleman."

He was buried at Forest Lawn alongside his mother and his sisters, Juel and Minna. The services were private, as he requested. The Wallis crypt is a beautiful marble room with a large picture window overlooking the rolling green hills surrounding Warner Bros. Studio.

I know that his life, his spirit, continues on in its same intelligence and wisdom—his body was only a vehicle of his consciousness. Consciousness rejoins consciousness. It is just no longer in this particular environment. What we knew was not the final form of his being. But, oh, how I miss that form.

9

BEGINNING AGAIN

I no longer wanted to live without Hal in the surroundings we'd shared or in the social situations we'd enjoyed. Too many memories, happy and sad.

I moved out of our homes in California as fast as I could and settled in Santa Fe, the City of the Holy Faith. Hal would approve. He loved this country.

As did D. H. Lawrence, who wrote:

> I think New Mexico was the greatest experience from the outside world that I have ever had. It certainly changed me forever. . . . The moment I saw the brilliant, proud morning shine high up over the deserts of Santa Fe, something stood still in my soul, and I started to attend.

Georgia O'Keeffe warned, "If you ever go to New Mexico it will itch you for the rest of your life."

It's true. This country casts its spell, and it never lets go. Like Africa. Hispanics call it *querencia*—a home for the heart.

Willa Cather in *Death Comes for the Archbishop* tells of the archbishop's early morning realization in New Mexico: "His first consciousness was a sense of the light dry wind blowing through the windows with the fragrance of hot sun and sagebrush and sweet clover. A wind that makes one's body feel light and one's heart cry 'Today. Today.' Like a child's."

I awaken each morning with the same cry—with zest, excitement, and enthusiasm, anticipating the very special quality of my days here.

Summer nights, I sleep out on my deck under the stars. Snowbound, I read and watch television in front of a piñon-log fire with my two comfortable cats, Morris and Smokey. I am surrounded by pine trees and the snow-covered peaks of the Sangre de Cristo Mountains. I enjoy fresh, crystal-pure air, electric-blue skies, unbelievable sunrises and sunsets.

In this mystical country, I have found my *hózhó*—the Navajo word meaning being in harmony with one's environment, at peace with one's circumstances, content with the day, devoid of anger, free from anxieties.

Unpacking boxes of Hollywood memorabilia recently, I found several photographs of a girl I once knew there. I've tried to forget her. She came on too strong to suit me, was bossy, stubborn, often devious. She hurt me deeply many, many times—others too.

But my perspective has changed now. From the vantage point of Oneness, I can view her with compassion and understanding. She made lots of mistakes in her life. Everybody does. But if God's love is all-forgiving, shouldn't ours be, too? I forgive her.

The girl in the photographs was me.

I released the past when I came to Santa Fe and brought only the good from lessons learned into the present. I still have problems to overcome, still experience occasional drops from cloud nine to cloud one or two, am still "under construction." But I no longer want to compete with anyone for anything. I don't envy anyone, am no longer interested in social position or things.

When old friends from California telephone me, the conversation usually goes something like this:

"Do you have any beaus?"

"No, I'm not in that business anymore."

"Well, what do you *do*?"

"I write, paint, walk, read, meditate, enjoy getting reacquainted with my own family. Out of the rat race at last."

Long Pause.

"What rat race?"

Not wanting to negate anybody's life-style or explain why I am no longer a player in the game, I change the subject.

The last verse of my song has not yet been sung, but it is from here that I will sing it. At one time, Santa Fe was the end of the trail. For me, it is the beginning—the beginning of a meaningful new life.

My goal? To live so that others see Him in me and are led to seek the same peace and fulfillment in a God-experience of their own.

When I was a little girl in Fort Worth, Texas, my father used to take me for a walk around the block every night after he got home from work. As we strode briskly along, he philosophized and advised. The counseling that molded my life was his inspiration to "be Somebody."

He told me how fortunate I was to be creative—that creativity was the greatest gift in life, kinship with the Almighty. "Leave something of value behind when you go, Marty," he urged, "something with your imagination and your name on it. The printed word lives, paintings live, film lives. All that we know of the past is what artists and writers and poets have left us. So make something of the talents you've been given. Be all that you can. Dream. Dare. Rise above the crowd. Let the world know you've passed by. Be Somebody."

Pop, I made it.

But worldly success brought little satisfaction. It took the harsh lessons of a lifetime to teach me that the only achievement that really counts is making contact with the spark of God within us, that love and surrender, not ambition, are the Keys to the Kingdom.

The great truth I learned is that every living thing is connected, part of a universal God Energy—one soul, one self, one spirit. Oneness is our true reality.

And we're all Somebody to Him.

FILMOGRAPHY

The Locket, RKO, 1946
Thunder Mountain, RKO, 1947
The Velvet Touch, RKO, 1948
Gun Smugglers, RKO, 1949
The Judge Steps Out, RKO, 1949
Roughshod, RKO, 1949
Rustlers, RKO, 1949
The Lawless, Paramount, 1950
Outcast of Black Mesa, Columbia, 1950
Salt Lake Raiders, Republic, 1950
Frisco Tornado, Republic, 1950
Wild Stallion, Monogram, 1952
Yukon Gold, Monogram, 1952
Unmei-Fate, Breakston-Stahl Productions, 1952
Geisha Girl, Breakston-Stahl Productions, 1952
Battle of Rogue River, Columbia, 1952
Abbott & Costello Go to Mars, Universal, 1953
Scarlet Spear, United Artists, 1953
So Big, Warner Bros., 1953
Riders to the Stars, United Artists, 1954
Lucky Me, Warner Bros., 1954
Cry Vengeance, Allied Artists, 1954
Down Three Dark Streets, United Artists, 1954
Sabrina, Paramount, 1954
Wyoming Renegades, Columbia, 1955
Kiss of Fire, Universal, 1955
Francis in the Navy, Universal, 1955
Fresh from Paris (also titled *Paris Follies of 1956*), Allied Artists, 1955

Red Sundown, Universal, 1956
Showdown at Abilene, Universal, 1956
The Delicate Delinquent, Paramount, 1957
Mister Cory, Universal, 1957
Kelly and Me, Universal, 1957
Battle Hymn, Universal, 1957
My Man Godfrey, Universal, 1957
Once Upon a Horse, Universal, 1958
Paris Holiday, United Artists, 1958
Houseboat, Paramount, 1958
Some Came Running, MGM, 1958
The Best of Everything, 20th Century Fox, 1959
The Big Fisherman, Buena Vista, 1959
Mistress of the World, CCC Productions, Munich, 1959
Desire in the Dust, 20th Century Fox, 1960
Ice Palace, Warner Bros., 1960
The Right Approach, 20th Century Fox, 1961
The Last Time I Saw Archie, United Artists, 1961
A Girl Named Tamiko, Paramount, 1962
Pyro, American International Pictures, 1963
Wives and Lovers, Paramount, 1963
The Man from the Diner's Club, Columbia, 1963
Blood on the Arrow, Allied Artists, 1964
The Carpetbaggers, Paramount, 1964
Bikini Beach, American International Pictures, 1964
First Men in the Moon, Columbia, 1964
Cuernavaca en Primavera, Producciones Bueno, Mexico City, 1965
The Sons of Katie Elder, Paramount, 1965
The Chase, Columbia, 1966
The Night of the Grizzly, Paramount, 1966
Picture Mommy Dead, Embassy, 1966
The Happening, Columbia, 1967
Some May Live (also titled *In Saigon, Some May Live*), Phil Krasna Productions/RKO, 1967
War, Italian Style, American International Pictures, 1967

Filmography

Another Man's Wife, Gil Productions, Madrid, 1968
Catch as Catch Can, Gassman Films, Rome, 1968
House of 1,000 Dolls, American International Pictures, 1968
Once You Kiss a Stranger, Warner Bros., 1969
Crossplot, EMI, London, 1970